插图珍藏本

十四行诗

The Sonnets

[英]莎士比亚（Shakespeare, W.）◎著

梁宗岱◎译

湖南文艺出版社
HUNAN LITERATURE AND ART PUBLISHING HOUSE

博集天卷
CS-BOOKY

图书在版编目（CIP）数据

十四行诗/（英）莎士比亚（Shakespeare，W.）著；
梁宗岱译.—长沙：湖南文艺出版社，2011.7
书名原文：The Sonnets
ISBN 978-7-5404-4925-4

Ⅰ.①十…　Ⅱ.①莎…②梁…　Ⅲ.①十四行诗－
诗集－英国－中世纪　Ⅳ.①I561.23

中国版本图书馆CIP数据核字（2011）第073699号

上架建议：青少年阅读·经典名著

十四行诗

作　　者：（英）莎士比亚（Shakespeare，W.）
译　　者：梁宗岱
出 版 人：刘清华
责任编辑：易　见　耿会芬
监　　制：吴成玮
策划编辑：耿金丽
版式设计：付　莉
封面设计：张丽娜
出版发行：湖南文艺出版社
　　　　　（长沙市雨花区东二环一段508号　邮编：410014）
网　　址：www.hnwy.net
印　　刷：北京嘉业印刷厂
经　　销：新华书店
开　　本：880×1230　1/32
字　　数：160千字
印　　张：10.5
版　　次：2011年7月第1版
印　　次：2017年6月第6次印刷
书　　号：ISBN 978-7-5404-4925-4
定　　价：26.00元

质量监督电话：010-59096394
团购电话：010-59320018

甜蜜的莎士比亚

1609年，四十五岁的莎士比亚，已经创作了很多令他声名鹊起的剧作。这一年，一本题为《莎士比亚十四行诗》的小书，出现在伦敦的书店里。詹姆士一世时代的伦敦人，走出教堂，花上几便士，就可买到这本含有154首十四行诗和一首题为《爱人的怨诉》的长诗的书。

显然，这本书的第一组即前126首诗，是写给一个俊美的年轻男士的。这些诗里面所关注的东西是多样的，有贵族气质、生育后代、性的背叛、诗歌、艺术、死亡以及时间的劫掠一切的力量等。从第127首到152首，诗中的重点，就从年轻男士转移到一位迷人却不忠的黑肤女人身上。里面写到了她的魅力、诗人对她的迷恋，以及后来当发现她的背叛后，诗人对她的厌憎和痛苦。大多数读者认为，这些十四行诗，跟写给那位年轻男士的诗，是互相关联的。

十四行诗是源于意大利民间的一种抒情短诗，文艺复兴初期曾盛行于整个欧洲。莎士比亚是英国十四行诗的代表人物，他的诗打破原有诗体的惯例，独树一帜，被称为"莎体"。对诗人而言，诗的结构越严谨就越难抒情，而莎士比亚的十四行诗却毫不拘谨，自由奔放，正如他的剧作天马行空，其诗歌的语言也富于想象，充满感情。

这是莎士比亚在世时唯一一部诗集，历来是文学爱好者们不得不看的文学名著。而对于那些狂热的莎士比亚崇拜者来说，"莎士比亚十四行诗"无疑也是接近诗人的最佳途径。英国19世纪"湖畔派"诗人华兹华斯说："用这把钥匙，莎士比亚打开了自己的心扉。"

Sonnet 1

From fairest creatures we desire increase,

That thereby beauty's rose might never die,

But as the riper should by time decease,

His tender heir might bear his memory;

But thou[①], contracted to thine own bright eyes,

Feed'st[②] thy light's flame with self-substantial fuel,

Making a famine where abundance lies,

Thyself thy foe, to thy sweet self too cruel.

Thou that art now the world's fresh ornament

And only herald to the gaudy spring,

Within thine own bud buriest thy content

And, tender churl, mak'st waste in niggarding.

Pity the world, or else this glutton be,

To eat the world's due, by the grave and thee.

① thou, thy, thee, thine: 在伊丽莎白时代，第二人称代词单数常用thou（主格，相当于you），其变格形式为thee（宾格，相当于you）、thy（所有格，相当于your）、thine（所有格，用于以元音或h开始的词前，相当于your；物主代词，相当于yours）、thyself（反身代词，相当于yourself）。

② feed'st, art, buriest, mak'st: 在早期现代英语中，几乎在thou后面的所有动词词尾形式都为-est, -st或-t. 在诗中feed'st=feed, art=are, buriest=bury, mak'st=make.

一

对天生的尤物我们要求蕃盛，
以便美的玫瑰永远不会枯死，
但开透的花朵既要及时凋零，
就应把记忆交给娇嫩的后嗣。

但你，只和你自己的明眸定情，
把自己当燃料喂养眼中的火焰，
和自己作对，待自己未免太狠，
把一片丰沃的土地变成荒田。

你现在是大地的清新的点缀，
又是锦绣阳春的唯一的前锋，
为什么把富源葬送在嫩蕊里，
温柔的鄙夫，要吝啬，反而浪用？

可怜这个世界吧，要不然，贪夫，
就吞噬世界的份，由你和坟墓。

Sonnet 2

When forty winters shall besiege thy brow,
And dig deep trenches in thy beauty's field,
Thy youth's proud livery, so gazed on now,
Will be a tattered weed of small worth held.

Then being asked, where all thy beauty lies,
Where all the treasure of thy lusty days,
To say, within thine own deep sunken eyes,
Were an all-eating shame, and thriftless praise.

How much more praise deserved thy beauty's use,
If thou couldst answer 'This fair child of mine
Shall sum my count, and make my old excuse,'
Proving his beauty by succession thine!

This were to be new made when thou art old,
And see thy blood warm when thou feel'st it cold.

二

当四十个冬天围攻你的朱颜，
在你美的园地挖下深的战壕，
你青春的华服，那么被人艳羡，
将成褴褛的败絮，谁也不要瞧。

那时人若问起你的美在何处，
哪里是你那少壮年华的宝藏，
你说，"在我这双深陷的眼眶里，
是贪婪的羞耻，和无益的颂扬。"

你的美的用途会更值得赞美，
如果你能够说，"我这宁馨小童
将总结我的账，宽恕我的老迈"，
证实他的美在继承你的血统！

这将使你在衰老的暮年更生，
并使你垂冷的血液感到重温。

Sonnet 3

Look in thy glass, and tell the face thou viewest
Now is the time that face should form another,
Whose fresh repair if now thou not renewest,
Thou dost beguile the world, unbless some mother.

For where is she so fair whose uneared womb
Disdains the tillage of thy husbandry?
Or who is he so fond will be the tomb
Of his self-love, to stop posterity?

Thou art thy mother's glass, and she in thee
Calls back the lovely April of her prime,
So thou through windows of thine age shalt see
Despite of wrinkles this thy golden time.

But if thou live, remembered not to be,
Die single, and thine image dies with thee.

三

照照镜子，告诉你那镜中的脸庞，
说现在这庞儿应该另造一副；
如果你不赶快为它重修殿堂，
就欺骗世界，剥掉母亲的幸福。

因为哪里会有女人那么淑贞，
她那处女的胎不愿被你耕种？
哪里有男人那么蠢，他竟甘心
做自己的坟墓，绝自己的血统？

你是你母亲的镜子，在你里面
她唤回她的盛年的芳菲四月；
同样，从你暮年的窗你将眺见——
纵皱纹满脸——你这黄金的岁月。

但是你活着若不愿被人惦记，
就独自死去，你的肖像和你一起。

Sonnet 4

Unthrifty loveliness, why dost thou spend

Upon thyself thy beauty's legacy?

Nature's bequest gives nothing, but doth[①] lend,

And being frank, she lends to those are free.

Then, beauteous niggard, why dost thou abuse

The bounteous largess given thee to give?

Profitless usurer, why dost thou use

So great a sum of sums, yet canst not live?

For having traffic with thyself alone,

Thou of thyself thy sweet self dost deceive,

Then how when nature calls thee to be gone,

What acceptable audit canst thou leave?

Thy unused beauty must be tombed with thee,

Which, used, lives th' executor to be.

---

① 〈古〉do的第三人称单数。

四

俊俏的浪子，为什么把你那份
美的遗产在你自己身上耗尽？
造化的馈赠非赐予，她只出赁；
她慷慨，只赁给宽宏大量的人。

那么，美丽的鄙夫，为什么滥用
那交给你转交给别人的厚礼？
赔本的高利贷者，为什么浪用
那么一笔大款，还不能过日子？

因为你既然只和自己做买卖，
就等于欺骗你那妩媚的自我。
这样，你将拿什么账目去交代，
当造化唤你回到她怀里长卧？

你未用过的美将同你进坟墓；
用呢，就活着去执行你的遗嘱。

Sonnet 5

Those hours, that with gentle work did frame

The lovely gaze where every eye doth dwell,

Will play the tyrants to the very same

And that unfair which fairly doth excel;

For never-resting time leads summer on

To hideous winter, and confounds him there;

Sap checked with frost, and lusty leaves quite gone,

Beauty o'er-snowed, and bareness everywhere.

Then were not summer's distillation left,

A liquid prisoner pent in walls of glass,

Beauty's effect with beauty were bereft,

Nor it nor no remembrance what it was.

But flowers distilled, though they with winter meet,

Lose but their show; their substance still lives sweet.

五

那些时辰曾经用轻盈的细工
织就这众目共注的可爱明眸，
终有天对它摆出魔王的面孔，
把绝代佳丽剜成龙钟的老丑。

因为不舍昼夜的时光把盛夏
带到狰狞的冬天去把它结果；
生机被严霜窒息，绿叶又全下，
白雪掩埋了美，满目是赤裸裸。

那时候如果夏天尚未经提炼，
让它凝成香露锁在玻璃瓶里，
美和美的流泽将一起被截断，
美，和美的记忆都无人再提起。

但提炼过的花，纵和冬天抗衡，
只失掉颜色，却永远吐着清芬。

Sonnet 6

Then let not winter's ragged hand deface,

In thee thy summer, ere thou be distilled:

Make sweet some vial; treasure thou some place

With beauty's treasure ere it be self-killed.

That use is not forbidden usury,

Which happies those that pay the willing loan;

That's for thyself to breed another thee,

Or ten times happier, be it ten for one;

Ten times thyself were happier than thou art,

If ten of thine ten times refigured thee.

Then what could death do if thou shouldst depart,

Leaving thee living in posterity?

Be not self-willed, for thou art much too fair

To be death's conquest and make worms thine heir.

六

那么，别让冬天嶙峋的手抹掉
你的夏天，在你未经提炼之前，
熏香一些瓶子；把你美的财宝
藏在宝库里，趁它还未及消散。

这样的借贷并不是违禁取利，
既然它使那乐意纳息的高兴；
这是说你该为你另生一个你，
或者，一个生十，就十倍地幸运；

十倍你自己比你现在更快乐，
如果你有十个儿子来重现你。
这样，即使你长辞，死将奈你何，
既然你继续活在你的后裔里？

别任性：你那么标致，何必甘心
做死的胜利品，让蛆虫做子孙。

Sonnet 7

Lo, in the orient when the gracious light
Lifts up his burning head, each under eye
Doth homage to his new-appearing sight,
Serving with looks his sacred majesty,

And having climbed the steep-up heavenly hill,
Resembling strong youth in his middle age,
Yet mortal looks adore his beauty still,
Attending on his golden pilgrimage.

But when from highmost pitch with weary car,
Like feeble age, he reeleth from the day,
The eyes, 'fore duteous, now converted are
From his low tract and look another way.

So thou, thyself out-going in thy noon,
Unlooked on diest, unless thou get a son.

七

看，当普照万物的太阳从东方
抬起了火红的头，下界的眼睛
都对他初升的景象表示敬仰，
用目光来恭候他神圣的驾临；

然后他既登上了苍穹的极峰，
像精力饱满的壮年，雄姿英发，
万民的眼睛依旧膜拜他的峥嵘，
紧紧追随着他那疾驰的金驾。

但当他，像耄年拖着尘倦的车轮，
从绝顶颤巍巍地离开了白天，
众目便一齐从他下沉的足印
移开它们那原来恭顺的视线。

同样，你的灿烂的日中一消逝，
你就会悄悄死去，如果没后嗣。

Sonnet 8

Music to hear, why hear'st thou music sadly?

Sweets with sweets war not, joy delights in joy.

Why lov'st thou that which thou receiv'st not gladly,

Or else receiv'st with pleasure thine annoy?

If the true concord of well-tuned sounds,

By unions married, do offend thine ear,

They do but sweetly chide thee, who confounds

In singleness the parts that thou shouldst bear.

Mark how one string, sweet husband to another,

Strikes each in each by mutual ordering;

Resembling sire, and child, and happy mother,

Who, all in one, one pleasing note do sing;

Whose speechless song being many, seeming one,

Sings this to thee, 'Thou single wilt prove none'.

八

我的音乐，为何听音乐会生悲？
甜蜜不相克，快乐使快乐欢笑。
为何爱那你不高兴爱的东西，
或者为何乐于接受你的烦恼？

如果悦耳的声音的完美和谐
和亲挚的协调会惹起你烦忧，
它们不过委婉地责备你不该
用独奏窒息你心中那部合奏。

试看这一根弦，另一根的良人，
怎样融洽地互相呼应和振荡；
宛如父亲、儿子和快活的母亲，
它们联成了一片，齐声在欢唱。

它们的无言之歌都异曲同工
对你唱着："你独身就一切皆空。"

Sonnet 9

Is it for fear to wet a widow's eye

That thou consum'st thyself in single life?

Ah, if thou issueless shalt hap to die,

The world will wail thee, like a makeless wife;

The world will be thy widow and still weep

That thou no form of thee hast left behind,

When every private widow well may keep

By children's eyes her husband's shape in mind.

Look, what an unthrift in the world doth spend

Shifts but his place, for still the world enjoys it;

But beauty's waste hath[①] in the world an end,

And kept unused, the user so destroys it.

No love toward others in that bosom sits

That on himself such murd'rous shame commits.

---

① 〈古〉have的第三人称单数现在式。即现在的has。

九

是否因为怕打湿你寡妇的眼，
你在独身生活里消磨你自己？
哦，如果你不幸无后离开人间，
世界就要哀哭你，像丧偶的妻。

世界将是你寡妇，她永远伤心
你生前没给她留下你的容貌；
其他的寡妇，靠儿女们的眼睛，
反能把良人的肖像在心里长保。

看吧，浪子在世上的种种浪费
只换了主人，世界仍然在享受；
但美的消耗在人间将有终尾，
留着不用，就等于任由它腐朽。

这样的心绝不会对别人有爱，
既然它那么忍心把自己戕害。

Sonnet 10

For shame deny that thou bear'st love to any,

Who for thyself art so unprovident.

Grant, if thou wilt, thou art beloved of many,

But that thou none lov'st is most evident;

For thou art so possessed with murd'rous hate,

That 'gainst thyself thou stick'st not to conspire,

Seeking that beauteous roof to ruinate

Which to repair should be thy chief desire.

O! change thy thought, that I may change my mind,

Shall hate be fairer lodged than gentle love?

Be, as thy presence is, gracious and kind,

Or to thyself at least kind-hearted prove:

Make thee another self for love of me,

That beauty still may live in thine or thee.

一〇

羞呀，否认你并非不爱任何人，
对待你自己却那么欠缺绸缪。
承认，随你便，许多人对你钟情，
但说你并不爱谁，谁也要点头。

因为怨毒的杀机那么缠住你，
你不惜多方设计把自己戕害，
锐意摧残你那座峥嵘的殿宇，
你唯一念头却该是把它重盖。

哦，赶快回心吧，让我也好转意！
难道憎比温婉的爱反得处优？
你那么貌美，愿你也一样心慈，
否则至少对你自己也要温柔。

另造一个你吧，你若是真爱我，
让美在你儿子或你身上永活。

Sonnet 11

As fast as thou shalt wane, so fast thou grow'st
In one of thine, from that which thou departest,
And that fresh blood which youngly thou bestow'st
Thou mayst call thine, when thou from youth convertest.

Herein lives wisdom, beauty, and increase,
Without this folly, age, and cold decay;
If all were minded so, the times should cease,
And threescore year would make the world away.

Let those whom nature hath not made for store,
Harsh, featureless, and rude, barrenly perish.
Look whom she best endowed, she gave thee more,
Which bounteous gift thou shouldst in bounty cherish.

She carved thee for her seal, and meant thereby
Thou shouldst print more, not let that copy die.

一一

和你一样快地消沉，你的儿子
也将一样快在世界生长起来；
你灌注给青春的这新鲜血液
仍将是你的，当青春把你抛开。

这里面活着智慧、美丽和昌盛，
没有这，便是愚蠢、衰老和腐朽。
人人都这样想，就要钟停漏尽，
六十年便足使世界化为乌有。

让那些人生来不配生育传宗，
粗鲁、丑陋和笨拙，无后地死去；
造化的至宠，她的馈赠也最丰，
该尽量爱惜她这慷慨的赐予。

她把你刻做她的印，意思是要
你多印几份，并非要毁掉原稿。

Sonnet 12

When I do count the clock that tells the time,

And see the brave day sunk in hideous night,

When I behold the violet past prime,

And sable curls all silvered o'er with white;

When lofty trees I see barren of leaves,

Which erst from heat did canopy the herd,

And summer's green all girded up in sheaves

Borne on the bier with white and bristly beard:

Then of thy beauty do I question make

That thou among the wastes of time must go,

Since sweets and beauties do themselves forsake,

And die as fast as they see others grow;

And nothing 'gainst Time's scythe can make defence,

Save breed to brave him, when he takes thee hence.

一二

当我数着壁上报时的自鸣钟，
见明媚的白昼坠入狰狞的夜，
当我凝望着紫罗兰老了春容，
青丝的卷发遍洒着皑皑白雪；

当我看见参天的树枝叶尽脱，
它不久前曾荫蔽喘息的牛羊；
夏天的青翠一束一束地就缚，
带着坚挺的白须被舁上殓床；

于是我不禁为你的朱颜焦虑：
终有天你要加入时光的废堆。
既然美和芳菲都把自己抛弃，
眼看着别人生长自己却枯萎。

没什么抵挡得住时光的毒手，
除了生育，当他来要把你拘走。

Sonnet 13

O, that you were yourself, but, love, you are

No longer yours, than you yourself here live.

Against this coming end you should prepare,

And your sweet semblance to some other give.

So should that beauty which you hold in lease

Find no determination, then you were

Yourself again after yourself's decease,

When your sweet issue your sweet form should bear.

Who lets so fair a house fall to decay,

Which husbandry in honour might uphold,

Against the stormy gusts of winter's day

And barren rage of death's eternal cold?

O, none but unthrifts; dear my love, you know,

You had a father, let your son say so.

一三

哦，但愿你是你自己，但爱呀，你
终非你有，当你不再活在世上。
对这将临的日子你得要准备，
快交给别人你那俊秀的肖像。

这样，你所租赁的朱颜就永远
不会有满期；于是你又将变成
你自己，当你已经离开了人间，
既然你儿子保留着你的倩影。

谁肯让一座这样的华厦倾颓，
如果小心地看守便可以维护
它的光彩，去抵抗隆冬的狂吹
和那冷酷的死神无情的暴怒？

哦，除非是浪子。我爱呀，你知道
你有父亲，让你儿子也可自豪。

Sonnet 14

Not from the stars do I my judgement pluck,

And yet methinks I have astronomy,

But not to tell of good, or evil luck,

Of plagues, of dearths, or seasons' quality.

Nor can I fortune to brief minutes tell;

'Pointing to each his thunder, rain and wind,

Or say with princes if it shall go well

By oft predict that I in heaven find.

But from thine eyes my knowledge I derive,

And constant stars in them I read such art

As truth and beauty shall together thrive

If from thyself, to store thou wouldst convert.

Or else of thee this I prognosticate,

Thy end is truth's and beauty's doom and date.

一四

并非从星辰我采集我的推断；
可是我以为我也精通占星学，
但并非为了推算气运的通蹇，
以及饥荒、瘟疫或四时的风色。

我也不能为短促的时辰算命，
指出每个时辰的雷电和风雨，
或为国王占卜流年是否亨顺，
依据我常从上苍探得的天机。

我的术数只得自你那双明眸，
恒定的双星，它们预兆这吉祥：
只要你回心转意肯储蓄传后，
真和美将双双偕你永世其昌。

要不然关于你我将这样昭示：
你的末日也就是真和美的死。

Sonnet 15

When I consider everything that grows
Holds in perfection but a little moment,
That this huge stage presenteth nought but shows
Whereon the stars in secret influence comment;

When I perceive that men as plants increase,
Cheered and checked even by the self-same sky;
Vaunt in their youthful sap, at height decrease,
And wear their brave state out of memory;

Then the conceit of this inconstant stay,
Sets you most rich in youth before my sight,
Where wasteful time debateth with decay
To change your day of youth to sullied night,

And all in war with Time for love of you,
As he takes from you, I engraft you new.

一五

当我默察一切活泼泼的生机
保持它们的芳菲都不过一瞬，
宇宙的舞台只搬弄一些把戏
被上苍的星宿在冥冥中牵引；

当我发觉人和草木一样蕃衍，
任同一的天把他鼓励和阻挠，
少壮时欣欣向荣，盛极又必反，
繁华和璀璨都被从记忆抹掉；

于是这一切奄忽浮生的征候
便把妙龄的你在我眼前呈列，
眼见残暴的时光与腐朽同谋，
要把你青春的白昼化作黑夜。

为了你的爱我将和时光争持：
他摧折你，我要把你重新接枝。

Sonnet 16

But wherefore do not you a mightier way

Make war upon this bloody tyrant Time?

And fortify yourself in your decay

With means more blessed than my barren rhyme?

Now stand you on the top of happy hours,

And many maiden gardens yet unset,

With virtuous wish would bear you living flowers,

Much liker than your painted counterfeit.

So should the lines of life that life repair

Which this Time's pencil or my pupil pen

Neither in inward worth nor outward fair

Can make you live yourself in eyes of men.

To give away yourself, keeps yourself still,

And you must live drawn by your own sweet skill.

一六

但是为什么不用更凶的法子
去抵抗这血淋淋的魔王——时光？
不用比我的枯笔吉利的武器，
去防御你的衰朽，把自己加强？

你现在站在黄金时辰的绝顶，
许多少女的花园，还未经播种，
贞洁地切盼你那绚烂的群英，
比你的画像更酷肖你的真容。

只有生命的线能把生命重描；
时光的画笔，或者我这枝弱管，
无论内心的美或外貌的姣好，
都不能使你在人们眼前活现。

献出你自己依然保有你自己，
而你得活着，靠你自己的妙笔。

Sonnet 17

Who will believe my verse in time to come

If it were filled with your most high deserts?

Though yet heaven knows it is but as a tomb

Which hides your life, and shows not half your parts.

If I could write the beauty of your eyes,

And in fresh numbers number all your graces,

The age to come would say this poet lies,

Such heavenly touches ne'er touched earthly faces.

So should my papers, yellowed with their age,

Be scorned, like old men of less truth than tongue,

And your true rights be termed a poet's rage,

And stretched metre of an antique song.

But were some child of yours alive that time,

You should live twice in it, and in my rhyme.

一七

未来的时代谁会相信我的诗，
如果它充满了你最高的美德?
虽然，天知道，它只是一座墓地
埋着你的生命和一半的本色。

如果我写得出你美目的流盼，
用清新的韵律细数你的秀妍，
未来的时代会说："这诗人撒谎：
这样的天姿哪里会落在人间！"

于是我的诗册，被岁月所熏黄，
就要被人藐视，像饶舌的老头；
你的真容被诬作诗人的疯狂，
以及一支古歌的夸张的节奏。

但那时你若有个儿子在人世，
你就活两次：在他身上，在诗里。

Sonnet 18

Shall I compare thee to a summer's day?

Thou art more lovely and more temperate.

Rough winds do shake the darling buds of May,

And summer's lease hath all too short a date.

Sometime too hot the eye of heaven shines,

And often is his gold complexion dimmed,

And every fair from fair sometime declines,

By chance, or nature's changing course untrimmed;

But thy eternal summer shall not fade,

Nor lose possession of that fair thou ow'st,

Nor shall death brag thou wand'rest in his shade,

When in eternal lines to time thou grow'st.

So long as men can breathe or eyes can see,

So long lives this, and this gives life to thee.

一八

我怎么能够把你来比作夏天？
你不独比它可爱也比它温婉。
狂风把五月宠爱的嫩蕊作践，
夏天出赁的期限又未免太短。

天上的眼睛有时照得太酷烈。
它那炳耀的金颜又常遭掩蔽。
被机缘或无常的天道所摧折，
没有芳艳不终于凋残或销毁。

但是你的长夏永远不会凋落，
也不会损失你这皎洁的红芳，
或死神夸口你在他影里漂泊，
当你在不朽的诗里与时同长。

只要一天有人类，或人有眼睛，
这诗将长存，并且赐给你生命。

Sonnet 19

Devouring Time blunt thou the lion's paws,

And make the earth devour her own sweet brood,

Pluck the keen teeth from the fierce tiger's jaws,

And burn the long-lived phoenix, in her blood;

Make glad and sorry seasons as thou fleet'st,

And do whate'er thou wilt, swift-footed Time,

To the wide world and all her fading sweets.

But I forbid thee one most heinous crime,

O, carve not with thy hours my love's fair brow,

Nor draw no lines there with thine antique pen,

Him in thy course untainted do allow,

For beauty's pattern to succeeding men.

Yet, do thy worst, old Time: despite thy wrong,

My love shall in my verse ever live young.

一九

饕餮的时光，去磨钝雄狮的爪，
命大地吞噬自己宠爱的幼婴，
去猛虎的颚下把它利牙拔掉，
焚毁长寿的凤凰，灭绝它的种，

使季节在你飞逝时或悲或喜；
而且，捷足的时光，尽肆意地摧残
这大千世界和它易谢的芳菲；
只有这极恶大罪我禁止你犯：

哦，别把岁月刻在我爱的额上，
或用古老的铁笔乱画下皱纹；
在你的飞逝里不要把它弄脏，
好留给后世永作美丽的典型。

但，尽管猖狂，老时光，凭你多狠，
我的爱在我诗里将万古长青。

Sonnet 20

A woman's face with nature's own hand painted,

Hast thou the master-mistress of my passion,

A woman's gentle heart but not acquainted

With shifting change as is false women's fashion,

An eye more bright than theirs, less false in rolling,

Gilding the object whereupon it gazeth,

A man in hue all hues in his controlling,

Which steals men's eyes and women's souls amazeth.

And for a woman wert thou first created,

Till nature as she wrought thee fell a-doting,

And by addition me of thee defeated,

By adding one thing to my purpose nothing.

But since she pricked thee out for women's pleasure,

Mine be thy love and thy love's use their treasure.

二〇

你有副女人的脸，由造化亲手
塑就，你，我热爱的情妇兼情郎；
有颗女人的温婉的心，但没有
反复和变幻，像女人的假心肠；

眼睛比她明媚，又不那么造作，
流盼把一切事物都镀上黄金；
绝世的美色，驾御着一切美色，
既使男人晕眩，又使女人震惊。

开头原是把你当女人来创造：
但造化塑造你时，不觉着了迷，
误加给你一件东西，这就剥掉
我的权利——这东西对我毫无意义。

但造化造你既专为女人愉快，
让我占有，而她们享受，你的爱。

Sonnet 21

So is it not with me as with that muse,

Stirred by a painted beauty to his verse,

Who heaven itself for ornament doth use,

And every fair with his fair doth rehearse,

Making a couplement of proud compare

With sun and moon, with earth and sea's rich gems,

With April's first-born flowers and all things rare,

That heaven's air in this huge rondure hems.

O, let me true in love but truly write,

And then believe me, my love is as fair

As any mother's child, though not so bright

As those gold candles fixed in heaven's air.

Let them say more that like of hearsay well,

I will not praise that purpose not to sell.

二一

我的诗神①并不像那一位诗神
只知运用脂粉涂抹他的诗句,
连苍穹也要搬下来作妆饰品,
罗列每个佳丽去赞他的佳丽,

用种种浮夸的比喻作成对偶,
把他比太阳、月亮、海陆的瑰宝,
四月的鲜花,和这浩荡的宇宙
蕴藏在它的怀里的一切奇妙。

哦,让我既真心爱,就真心歌唱,
而且,相信我,我的爱可以媲美
任何母亲的儿子,虽然论明亮
比不上挂在天空的金色烛台。

谁喜欢空话,让他尽说个不穷;
我志不在出售,自用不着祷颂。

---

① 诗神:即诗人,故下面用男性代词"他"字。

Sonnet 22

My glass shall not persuade me I am old,

So long as youth and thou are of one date,

But when in thee time's furrows I behold,

Then look I death my days should expiate.

For all that beauty that doth cover thee

Is but the seemly raiment of my heart,

Which in thy breast doth live, as thine in me,

How can I then be elder than thou art?

O therefore love be of thyself so wary,

As I not for myself, but for thee will,

Bearing thy heart which I will keep so chary

As tender nurse her babe from faring ill.

Presume not on thy heart when mine is slain,

Thou gav'st me thine not to give back again.

二二

这镜子绝不能使我相信我老，
只要大好韶华和你还是同年；
但当你脸上出现时光的深槽，
我就盼死神来了结我的天年。

因为那一切妆点着你的美丽
都不过是我内心的表面光彩；
我的心在你胸中跳动，正如你
在我的。那么，我怎会比你先衰？

哦，我的爱呵，请千万自己珍重，
像我珍重自己，乃为你，非为我。
怀抱着你的心，我将那么郑重，
像慈母防护着婴儿遭受病魔。

别侥幸独存，如果我的心先碎；
你把心交我，并非为把它收回。

Sonnet 23

As an unperfect actor on the stage,

Who with his fear is put beside his part,

Or some fierce thing replete with too much rage,

Whose strength's abundance weakens his own heart;

So I for fear of trust, forget to say,

The perfect ceremony of love's rite,

And in mine own love's strength seem to decay,

O'ercharged with burthen of mine own love's might.

O let my books be then the eloquence,

And dumb presagers of my speaking breast,

Who plead for love, and look for recompense,

More than that tongue that more hath more expressed.

O learn to read what silent love hath writ,

To hear with eyes belongs to love's fine wit.

二三

仿佛舞台上初次演出的戏子
慌乱中竟忘记了自己的角色，
又像被触犯的野兽满腔怒气，
它那过猛的力量反使它胆怯；

同样，缺乏着冷静，我不觉忘掉
举行爱情的仪节的彬彬盛典，
被我爱情的过度重量所压倒，
在我自己的热爱中一息奄奄。

哦，请让我的诗篇做我的辩士，
替我把缠绵的衷曲默默诉说，
它为爱情申诉，并希求着赏赐，
多于那对你絮絮不休的狡舌。

请学会去读缄默的爱的情书，
用眼睛来听原属于爱的妙术。

Sonnet 24

Mine eye hath played the painter and hath steeled

Thy beauty's form in table of my heart,

My body is the frame wherein 'tis[①] held,

And perspective it is best painter's art.

For through the painter must you see his skill,

To find where your true image pictured lies,

Which in my bosom's shop is hanging still,

That hath his windows glazed with thine eyes.

Now see what good turns eyes for eyes have done,

Mine eyes have drawn thy shape, and thine for me

Are windows to my breast, where-through the sun

Delights to peep, to gaze therein on thee;

Yet eyes this cunning want to grace their art,

They draw but what they see, know not the heart.

---

① "it is" 的缩写，常用于诗歌。

二四

我眼睛扮作画家，把你的肖像
描画在我的心版上，我的肉体
就是那嵌着你的姣颜的镜框，
而画家的无上的法宝是透视。

你要透过画家的巧妙去发现
那珍藏你的奕奕真容的地方；
它长挂在我胸内的画室中间，
你的眼睛却是画室的玻璃窗。

试看眼睛多么会帮眼睛的忙：
我的眼睛画你的像，你的却是
开向我胸中的窗，从那里太阳
喜欢去偷看那藏在里面的你。

可是眼睛的艺术终欠这高明：
它只能画外表，却不认识内心。

Sonnet 25

Let those who are in favour with their stars

Of public honour and proud titles boast,

Whilst I, whom fortune of such triumph bars

Unlooked for joy in that I honour most.

Great princes' favourites their fair leaves spread,

But as the marigold at the sun's eye,

And in themselves their pride lies buried,

For at a frown they in their glory die.

The painful warrior famoused for fight,

After a thousand victories once foiled,

Is from the book of honour razed quite,

And all the rest forgot for which he toiled.

Then happy I, that love and am beloved,

Where I may not remove nor be removed.

二五

让那些人（他们既有吉星高照）
到处夸说他们的显位和高官，
至于我，命运拒绝我这种荣耀，
只暗中独自赏玩我心里所欢。

王公的宠臣舒展他们的金叶
不过像太阳眷顾下的金盏花，
他们的骄傲在自己身上消灭，
一蹙额便足凋谢他们的荣华。

转战沙场的名将不管多功高，
百战百胜后只要有一次失手，
便从功名册上被人一笔勾销，
毕生的勋劳只落得无声无臭。

那么，爱人又被爱，我多么幸福！
我既不会迁徙，又不怕被驱逐。

Sonnet 26

Lord of my love, to whom in vassalage

Thy merit hath my duty strongly knit;

To thee I send this written embassage,

To witness duty, not to show my wit.

Duty so great, which wit so poor as mine

May make seem bare, in wanting words to show it;

But that I hope some good conceit of thine

In thy soul's thought, all naked, will bestow it,

Till whatsoever star that guides my moving,

Points on me graciously with fair aspect,

And puts apparel on my tattered loving,

To show me worthy of thy sweet respect.

Then may I dare to boast how I do love thee,

Till then, not show my head where thou mayst prove me.

二六

我爱情的至尊，你的美德已经
使我这藩属加强对你的拥戴，
我现在寄给你这诗当作使臣，
去向你述职，并非要向你炫才。

职责那么重，我又才拙少俊语，
难免要显得赤裸裸和她相见，
但望你的妙思，不嫌它太粗鄙，
在你灵魂里把它的赤裸裸遮掩；

因而不管什么星照引我前程，
都对我露出一副和悦的笑容，
把华服加给我这寒伧的爱情，
使我配得上你那缱绻的恩宠。

那时我才敢对你夸耀我的爱，
否则怕你考验我，总要躲起来。

Sonnet 27

Weary with toil, I haste me to my bed,

The dear respose for limbs with travel tired,

But then begins a journey in my head

To work my mind, when body's work's expired.

For then my thoughts, from far where I abide,

Intend a zealous pilgrimage to thee,

And keep my drooping eyelids open wide,

Looking on darkness which the blind do see.

Save that my soul's imaginary sight,

Presents thy shadow to my sightless view,

Which like a jewel hung in ghastly night,

Makes black night beauteous, and her old face new.

Lo! thus, by day my limbs, by night my mind,

For thee, and for myself, no quiet find.

二七

精疲力竭，我赶快到床上躺下，
去歇息我那整天劳顿的四肢；
但马上我的头脑又整装出发，
以劳我的心，当我身已得休息。

因为我的思想，不辞离乡背井，
虔诚地趱程要到你那里进香，
睁大我这双沉沉欲睡的眼睛，
向着瞎子看得见的黑暗凝望；

不过我的灵魂，凭着它的幻眼，
把你的倩影献给我失明的双眸，
像颗明珠在阴森的夜里高悬，
变老丑的黑夜为明丽的白昼。

这样，日里我的腿，夜里我的心，
为你、为我自己，都得不着安宁。

Sonnet 28

How can I then return in happy plight
That am debarred the benefit of rest?
When day's oppression is not eased by night,
But day by night and night by day oppressed.

And each, though enemies to either's reign,
Do in consent shake hands to torture me,
The one by toil, the other to complain
How far I toil, still farther off from thee.

I tell the day to please him thou art bright,
And dost him grace when clouds do blot the heaven;
So flatter I the swart-complexioned night,
When sparkling stars twire not thou gild'st the even.

But day doth daily draw my sorrows longer,
And night doth nightly make grief's length seem stronger.

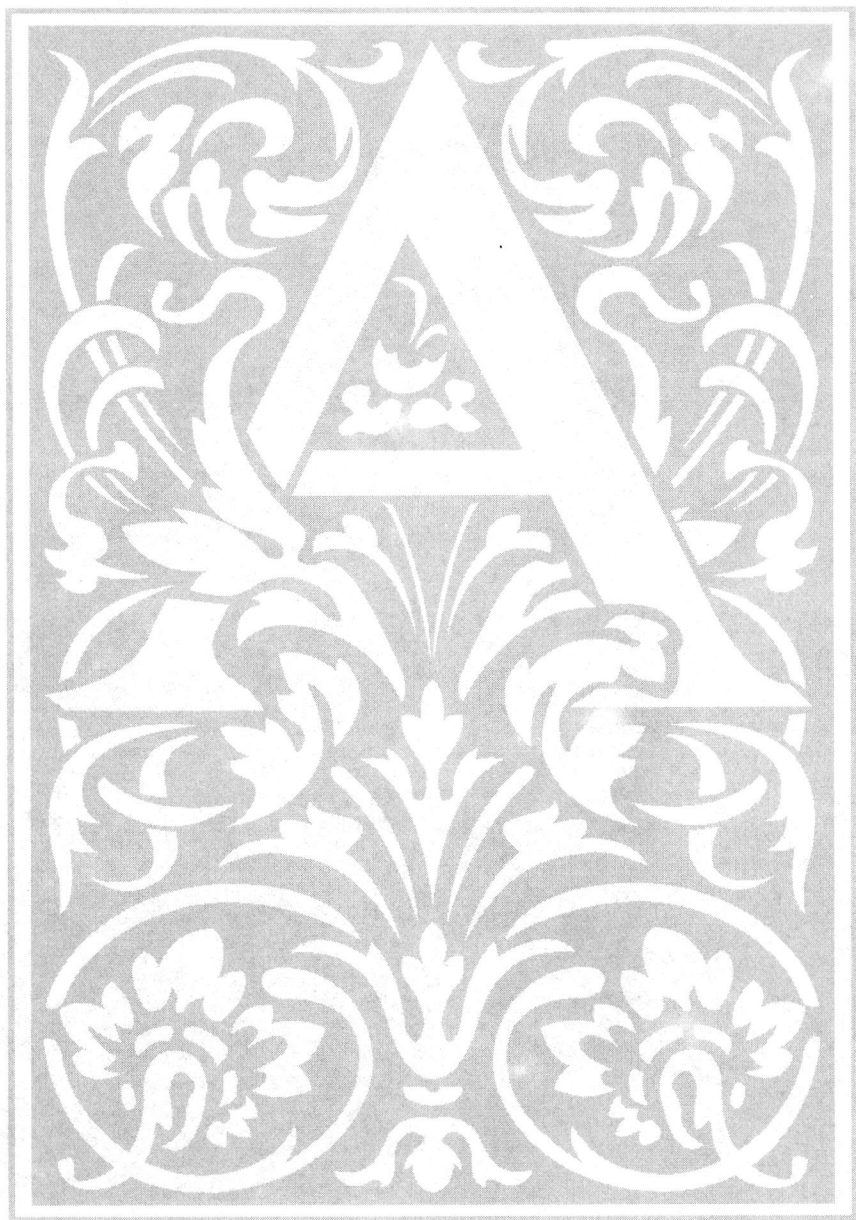

二八

那么，我怎么能够喜洋洋归来，
既然得不着片刻身心的安息？
当白天的压逼入夜并不稍衰，
只是夜继日、日又继夜地压逼？

日和夜平时虽事事各不相下，
却互相携手来把我轮流挫折，
一个用跋涉，一个却呶呶怒骂，
说我离开你更远，虽整天跋涉。

为讨好白天，我告它你是光明，
在阴云密布时你将把它映照。
我又这样说去讨黑夜的欢心：
当星星不眨眼，你将为它闪耀。

但天天白天尽拖长我的苦痛，
夜夜黑夜又使我的忧思转凶。

Sonnet 29

When in disgrace with Fortune and men's eyes,

I all alone beweep my outcast state,

And trouble deaf heaven with my bootless cries,

And look upon myself and curse my fate,

Wishing me like to one more rich in hope,

Featured like him, like him with friends possessed,

Desiring this man's art, and that man's scope,

With what I most enjoy contented least.

Yet in these thoughts myself almost despising,

Haply I think on thee, and then my state,

Like to the lark at break of day arising

From sullen earth, sings hymns at heaven's gate;

For thy sweet love remembered such wealth brings,

That then I scorn to change my state with kings.

二九

当我受尽命运和人们的白眼，
暗暗地哀悼自己的身世飘零，
徒用呼吁去干扰聋聩的昊天，
顾盼着身影，诅咒自己的生辰，

愿我和另一个一样富于希望，
面貌相似，又和他一样广交游，
希求这人的渊博，那人的内行，
最赏心的乐事觉得最不对头。

可是，当我正要这样看轻自己，
忽然想起了你，于是我的精神，
便像云雀破晓从阴霾的大地
振翅上升，高唱着圣歌在天门。

一想起你的爱使我那么富有，
和帝王换位我也不屑于屈就。

Sonnet 30

When to the sessions of sweet silent thought,

I summon up remembrance of things past,

I sigh the lack of many a thing I sought,

And with old woes new wail my dear time's waste.

Then can I drown an eye, unused to flow

For precious friends hid in death's dateless night,

And weep afresh love's long since cancelled woe,

And moan the expense of many a vanished sight.

Then can I grieve at grievances foregone,

And heavily from woe to woe tell o'er

The sad account of fore-bemoaned moan,

Which I new pay as if not paid before.

But if the while I think on thee , dear friend,

All losses are restored, and sorrows end.

三〇

当我传唤对已往事物的记忆
出庭于那馨香的默想的公堂，
我不禁为命中许多缺陷叹息，
带着旧恨，重新哭蹉跎的时光；

于是我可以淹没那枯涸的眼，
为了那些长埋在夜台的亲朋，
哀悼着许多音容俱渺的美艳，
痛哭那情爱久已勾销的哀痛；

于是我为过去的惆怅而惆怅，
并且一一细算，从痛苦到痛苦，
那许多呜咽过的呜咽的旧账，
仿佛还未付过，现在又来偿付。

但是只要那刻我想起你，挚友，
损失全收回，悲哀也化为乌有。

Sonnet 31

Thy bosom is endeared with all hearts,

Which I by lacking have supposed dead,

And there reigns love and all love's loving parts,

And all those friends which I thought buried.

How many a holy and obsequious tear

Hath dear religious love stol'n from mine eye,

As interest of the dead, which now appear

But things removed that hidden in thee lie!

Thou art the grave where buried love doth live,

Hung with the trophies of my lovers gone,

Who all their parts of me to thee did give,

That due of many, now is thine alone.

Their images I loved, I view in thee,

And thou, all they, hast all the all of me.

三一

你的胸怀有了那些心而越可亲
（它们的消逝我只道已经死去）；
原来爱，和爱的一切可爱部分，
和埋掉的友谊都在你怀里藏住。

多少为哀思而流的圣洁泪珠
那虔诚的爱曾从我眼睛偷取
去祭奠死者！我现在才恍然大悟
他们只离开我去住在你的心里。

你是座收藏已往恩情的芳塚，
满挂着死去的情人的纪念牌，
他们把我的馈赠尽向你呈贡，
你独自享受许多人应得的爱。

在你身上我瞥见他们的倩影，
而你，他们的总和，尽有我的心。

Sonnet 32

If thou survive my well-contented day,
When that churl death my bones with dust shall cover
And shalt by fortune once more re-survey
These poor rude lines of thy deceased lover,

Compare them with the bett'ring of the time,
And though they be outstripped by every pen,
Reserve them for my love, not for their rhyme,
Exceeded by the height of happier men.

O then vouchsafe me but this loving thought,
'Had my friend's Muse grown with this growing age,
A dearer birth than this his love had brought
To march in ranks of better equipage;

But since he died and poets better prove,
Theirs for their style I'll read, his for his love'.

三二

倘你活过我踌躇满志的大限，
当鄙夫"死神"用黄土把我掩埋，
偶然重翻这拙劣可怜的诗卷，
你情人生前写来献给你的爱，

把它和当代俊逸的新诗相比，
发觉它的词笔处处都不如人，
请保留它专为我的爱，而不是
为那被幸运的天才凌驾的韵。

哦，那时候就请赐给我这爱思：
"要是我朋友的诗神与时同长，
他的爱就会带来更美的产儿，
可和这世纪任何杰作同俯仰。

但他既死去，诗人们又都迈进，
我读他们的文采，却读他的心。"

Sonnet 33

Full many a glorious morning have I seen,

Flatter the mountain tops with sovereign eye,

Kissing with golden face the meadows green,

Gilding pale streams with heavenly alchemy;

Anon permit the basest clouds to ride

With ugly rack on his celestial face,

And from the forlorn world his visage hide,

Stealing unseen to west with this disgrace.

Even so my sun one early morn did shine,

With all triumphant splendour on my brow,

But out, alack, he was but one hour mine,

The region cloud hath masked him from me now.

Yet him for this, my love no whit disdaineth,

Suns of the world may stain, when heaven's sun staineth.

三三

多少次我曾看见灿烂的朝阳
用他那至尊的眼媚悦着山顶,
金色的脸庞吻着青碧的草场,
把黯淡的溪水镀成一片黄金;

然后蓦地任那最卑贱的云彩
带着黑影驰过他神圣的霁颜,
把他从这凄凉的世界藏起来,
偷移向西方去掩埋他的污点;

同样,我的太阳曾在一个清朝
带着辉煌的光华临照我前额;
但是唉!他只一刻是我的荣耀,
下界的乌云已把他和我遮隔。

我的爱却并不因此把他鄙贱,
天上的太阳有瑕疵,何况人间!

Sonnet 34

Why didst thou promise such a beauteous day,

And make me travel forth without my cloak,

To let base clouds o'ertake me in my way,

Hiding thy bravery in their rotten smoke?

'Tis not enough that through the cloud thou break,

To dry the rain on my storm-beaten face,

For no man well of such a salve can speak,

That heals the wound, and cures not the disgrace.

Nor can thy shame give physic to my grief,

Though thou repent, yet I have still the loss,

Th' offender's sorrow lends but weak relief

To him that bears the strong offence's cross.

Ah but those tears are pearl which thy love sheds,

And they are rich, and ransom all ill deeds.

三四

为什么预告那么璀璨的日子，
哄我不携带大衣便出来游行，
让鄙贱的乌云中途把我侵袭，
用臭腐的烟雾遮蔽你的光明？

你以为现在冲破乌云来晒干
我脸上淋漓的雨点便已满足？
须知无人会赞美这样的药丹，
只能医治创伤，但洗不了耻辱。

你的愧赧也无补于我的心疼，
你虽已忏悔，我依然不免损失。
对于背着耻辱的十字架的人，
冒犯者引咎只是微弱的慰藉。

唉，但你的爱所流的泪是明珠，
它们的富丽够赎你的罪有余。

Sonnet 35

No more be grieved at that which thou hast done,

Roses have thorns, and silver fountains mud,

Clouds and eclipses stain both moon and sun,

And loathsome canker lives in sweetest bud.

All men make faults, and even I in this,

Authorizing thy trespass with compare,

Myself corrupting salving thy amiss,

Excusing thy sins more than thy sins are;

For to thy sensual fault I bring in sense,

Thy adverse party is thy advocate,

And 'gainst myself a lawful plea commence:

Such civil war is in my love and hate,

That I an accessary needs must be,

To that sweet thief which sourly robs from me.

三五

别再为你冒犯我的行为痛苦：
玫瑰花有刺，银色的泉有烂泥，
乌云和蚀把太阳和月亮玷污，
可恶的毛虫把香的嫩蕊盘据。

每个人都有错，我就犯了这点：
运用种种比喻来解释你的恶，
弄脏我自己来洗涤你的罪愆，
赦免你那无可赦免的大错过。

因为对你的败行我加以谅解——
你的原告变成了你的辩护士——
我对你起诉，反而把自己出卖：
爱和憎老在我心中互相排挤，

以致我不得不变成你的助手
去帮你劫夺我，你，温柔的小偷！

Sonnet 36

Let me confess that we two must be twain,

Although our undivided loves are one;

So shall those blots that do with me remain,

Without thy help, by me be borne alone.

In our two loves there is but one respect,

Though in our lives a separable spite,

Which though it alter not love's sole effect,

Yet doth it steal sweet hours from love's delight.

I may not evermore acknowledge thee,

Lest my bewailed guilt should do thee shame,

Nor thou with public kindness honour me,

Unless thou take that honour from thy name.

But do not so, I love thee in such sort,

As thou being mine, mine is thy good report.

三六

让我承认我们俩一定要分离，
尽管我们那分不开的爱是一体。
这样，许多留在我身上的瑕疵，
将不用你分担，由我独自承起。

你我的相爱全出于一片至诚，
尽管不同的生活把我们隔开。
这纵然改变不了爱情的真纯，
却偷掉许多密约佳期的欢快。

我再也不会高声认你做知已，
生怕我可哀的罪过使你含垢；
你也不能再当众把我来赞美，
除非你甘心使你的名字蒙羞。

可别这样做。我既然这样爱你，
你是我的，我的荣光也属于你。

Sonnet 37

As a decrepit father takes delight

To see his active child do deeds of youth,

So I, made lame by Fortune's dearest spite,

Take all my comfort of thy worth and truth.

For whether beauty, birth, or wealth, or wit,

Or any of these all, or all, or more

Entitled in thy parts, do crowned sit,

I make my love engrafted to this store.

So then I am not lame, poor, nor despised,

Whilst that this shadow doth such substance give

That I in thy abundance am sufficed,

And by a part of all thy glory live.

Look what is best, that best I wish in thee:

This wish I have; then ten times happy me!

三七

像一个衰老的父亲高兴去看
活泼的儿子表演青春的伎俩，
同样，我，受了命运的恶毒摧残，
从你的精诚和美德找到力量。

因为，无论美、门第、财富或才华，
或这一切，或其一，或多于这一切，
在你身上登峰造极，我都把
我的爱在你这个宝藏上嫁接。

那么，我并不残废、贫穷、被轻蔑，
既然这种种幻影都那么充实，
使我从你的富裕得满足，并倚靠
你的光荣的一部分安然度日。

看，生命的至宝，我暗祝你尽有；
既有这心愿，我便十倍地无忧。

Sonnet 38

How can my muse want subject to invent,

While thou dost breathe that pour'st into my verse,

Thine own sweet argument, too excellent

For every vulgar paper to rehearse?

O! give thyself the thanks, if aught in me

Worthy perusal stand against thy sight;

For who's so dumb that cannot write to thee,

When thou thyself dost give invention light?

Be thou the tenth Muse, ten times more in worth

Than those old nine which rhymers invocate;

And he that calls on thee, let him bring forth

Eternal numbers to outlive long date.

If my slight muse do please these curious days,

The pain be mine, but thine shall be the praise.

三八

我的诗神怎么会找不到诗料，
当你还呼吸着，灌注给我的诗哦，
你自己的甜蜜主题——那么美妙
绝非世间俗笔所能描摹？①

感谢你自己吧，如果我诗中
有值得一读的献给你的目光。
哪里有哑巴，写到你，不善祷颂——
既然是你自己照亮他的想象？

做第十位艺神吧，你要比凡夫
所祈求的古代九位高明得多。
有谁向你呼吁，就让他献出
一些可以传久远的不朽诗歌。

我卑微的诗神如可取悦于世，
痛苦属于我，所有赞美全归你。

---

① 此处文字原稿缺失（第三、四行），由编者参考其他中译本补充。

Sonnet 39

O! how thy worth with manners may I sing,

When thou art all the better part of me?

What can mine own praise to mine own self bring,

And what is't but mine own when I praise thee?

Even for this, let us divided live,

And our dear love lose name of single one,

That by this separation I may give

That due to thee which thou deserv'st alone.

O absence! what a torment wouldst thou prove,

Were it not thy sour leisure gave sweet leave,

To entertain the time with thoughts of love,

Which time and thoughts so sweetly doth deceive.

And that thou teachest how to make one twain,

By praising him here who doth hence remain.

三九

哦，我怎能不越礼地把你歌颂，
当我的最优美部分全属于你？
赞美我自己对我自己有何用？
赞美你岂不等于赞美我自己？

就是为这点我们也得要分手，
使我们的爱名义上各自独处，
以便我可以，在这样分离之后，
把你该独得的赞美全部献出。

别离呵！你会给我多大的痛创，
倘若你辛酸的闲暇不批准我
拿出甜蜜的情思来款待时光，
用甜言把时光和相思蒙混过——

如果你不教我怎样化一为二，
使我在这里赞美远方的人儿！

Sonnet 40

Take all my loves, my love, yea take them all,

What hast thou then more than thou hadst before?

No love, my love, that thou mayst true love call,

All mine was thine, before thou hadst this more.

Then, if for my love, thou my love receivest,

I cannot blame thee, for my love thou usest,

But yet be blamed, if thou thyself deceivest

By wilful taste of what thyself refusest.

I do forgive thy robbery gentle thief,

Although thou steal thee all my poverty;

And yet love knows it is a greater grief

To bear greater wrong, than hate's known injury.

Lascivious grace, in whom all ill well shows,

Kill me with spites yet we must not be foes.

四〇

夺掉我的爱，爱呵，请通通夺去；
看看比你已有的能多些什么？
没什么，爱呵，称得上真情实义；
我所爱早属你，纵使不添这个。

那么，你为爱我而接受我所爱，
我不能对你这享受加以责备；
但得受责备，若甘心自我欺绐，
你故意贪尝不愿接受的东西。

我可以原谅你的掠夺，温柔贼，
虽然你把我仅有的通通偷走；
可是，忍受爱情的暗算，爱晓得，
比憎恨的明伤是更大的烦忧。

风流的妩媚，连你的恶也妩媚，
尽管毒杀我，我们可别相仇视。

Sonnet 41

Those pretty wrongs that liberty commits,

When I am sometime absent from thy heart,

Thy beauty, and thy years full well befits,

For still temptation follows where thou art.

Gentle thou art, and therefore to be won,

Beauteous thou art, therefore to be assailed.

And when a woman woos, what woman's son

Will sourly leave her till he have prevailed?

Ay me! but yet thou mightst my seat forbear,

And chide thy beauty, and thy straying youth,

Who lead thee in their riot even there

Where thou art forced to break a twofold troth:

Hers by thy beauty tempting her to thee,

Thine by thy beauty being false to me.

四一

你那放荡不羁所犯的风流罪
（当我有时候远远离开你的心）
与你的美貌和青春那么相配，
无论到哪里，诱惑都把你追寻。

你那么温文，谁不想把你夺取？
那么姣好，又怎么不被人围攻？
而当女人追求，凡女人的儿子
谁能坚苦挣扎，不向她怀里送？

唉！但你总不必把我的位儿占，
并斥责你的美丽和青春的迷惑。
它们引你去犯那么大的狂乱，
使你不得不撕毁了两重誓约：

她的，因为你的美诱她去就你；
你的，因为你的美对我失信义。

Sonnet 42

That thou hast her it is not all my grief,

And yet it may be said I loved her dearly,

That she hath thee is of my wailing chief,

A loss in love that touches me more nearly.

Loving offenders thus I will excuse ye[①] ,

Thou dost love her, because thou know'st I love her,

And for my sake even so doth she abuse me,

Suffering my friend for my sake to approve her.

If I lose thee, my loss is my love's gain,

And losing her, my friend hath found that loss,

Both find each other, and I lose both twain,

And both for my sake lay on me this cross.

But here's the joy, my friend and I are one,

Sweet flattery! then she loves but me alone.

---

① 〈古〉你；这，这个（=the）。

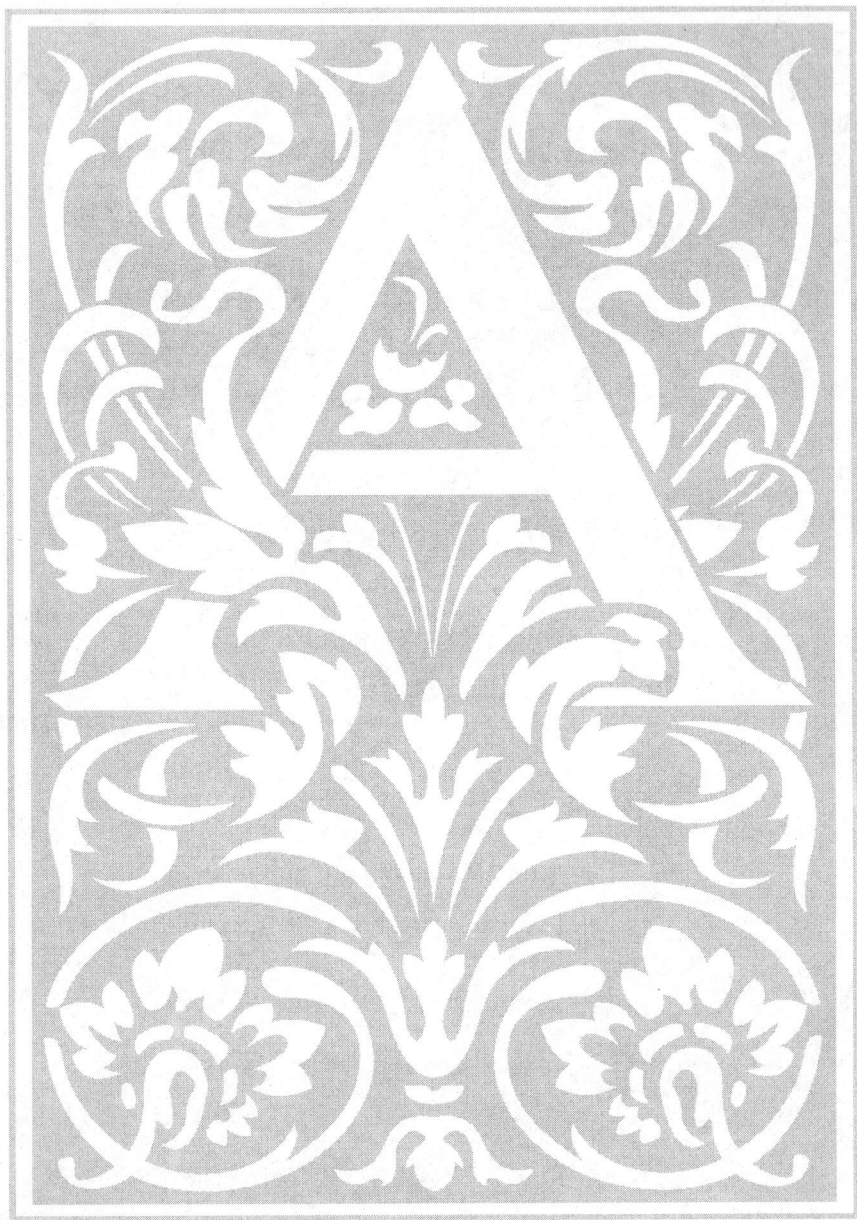

四二

你占有她，并非我最大的哀愁，
可是我对她的爱不能说不深；
她占有你，才是我主要的烦忧，
这爱情的损失更能使我伤心。

爱的冒犯者，我这样原谅你们：
你所以爱她，因为晓得我爱她；
也是为我的缘故她把我欺瞒，
让我的朋友替我殷勤款待她。

失掉你，我所失是我情人所获，
失掉她，我朋友却找着我所失；
你俩互相找着，而我失掉两个，
两个都为我的缘故把我磨折。

但这就是快乐：你和我是一体；
甜蜜的阿谀！她却只爱我自己。

Sonnet 43

When most I wink, then do mine eyes best see,

For all the day they view things unrespected,

But when I sleep, in dreams they look on thee,

And darkly bright, are bright in dark directed.

Then thou whose shadow shadows doth make bright,

How would thy shadow's form form happy show

To the clear day with thy much clearer light,

When to unseeing eyes thy shade shines so!

How would, I say, mine eyes be blessed made

By looking on thee in the living day,

When in dead night thy fair imperfect shade

Through heavy sleep on sightless eyes doth stay!

All days are nights to see till I see thee,

And nights bright days when dreams do show thee me.

四三

我眼睛闭得最紧，看得最明亮：
它们整天只看见无味的东西；
而当我入睡，梦中却向你凝望，
幽暗的火焰，暗地里放射幽辉。

你的影子既能教黑影放光明，
对闭上的眼照耀得那么辉煌，
你影子的形会形成怎样的美景，
在清明的白天里用更清明的光！

我的眼睛，我说，会感到多幸运
若能够凝望你在光天化日中，
既然在死夜里你那不完全的影
对酣睡中闭着的眼透出光容！

天天都是黑夜一直到看见你，
夜夜是白天当好梦把你显示！

Sonnet 44

If the dull substance of my flesh were thought,

Injurious distance should not stop my way,

For then despite of space I would be brought,

From limits far remote, where thou dost stay.

No matter then although my foot did stand

Upon the farthest earth removed from thee,

For nimble thought can jump both sea and land,

As soon as think the place where he would be.

But ah, thought kills me that I am not thought,

To leap large lengths of miles when thou art gone,

But that so much of earth and water wrought,

I must attend time's leisure with my moan.

Receiving nought by elements so slow,

But heavy tears, badges of either's woe.

四四

假如我这笨拙的体质是思想，
不做美的距离就不能阻止我，
因为我就会从那迢迢的远方，
无论多隔绝，被带到你的寓所。

那么，纵使我的腿站在那离你
最远的天涯，对我有什么妨碍？
空灵的思想无论想到达哪里，
它立刻可以飞越崇山和大海。

但是唉，这思想毒杀我：我并非思想，
能飞越辽远的万里当你去后；
而只是满盛着泥水的钝皮囊，
就只好用悲泣去把时光伺候；

这两种重浊的元素毫无所赐
除了眼泪，二者的苦恼的标志。

Sonnet 45

The other two, slight air, and purging fire

Are both with thee, wherever I abide,

The first my thought, the other my desire,

These present-absent with swift motion slide.

For when these quicker elements are gone

In tender embassy of love to thee,

My life being made of four, with two alone

Sinks down to death, oppressed with melancholy.

Until life's composition be recured

By those swift messengers returned from thee,

Who even but now come back again, assured

Of thy fair health, recounting it to me.

This told, I joy, but then no longer glad,

I send them back again, and straight grow sad.

四五

其余两种，轻清的风，净化的火，
一个是我的思想，一个是欲望，
都是和你一起，无论我居何所；
它们又在又不在，神速地来往。

因为，当这两种较轻快的元素
带着爱情的温柔使命去见你，
我的生命，本赋有四大，只守住
两个，就不胜其忧郁，奄奄待毙；

直到生命的结合得完全恢复
由于这两个敏捷使者的来归。
它们现正从你那里回来，欣悉
你起居康吉，在向我欣欣告慰。

说完了，我乐，可是并不很长久，
我打发它们回去，马上又发愁。

Sonnet 46

Mine eye and heart are at a mortal war,

How to divide the conquest of thy sight,

Mine eye, my heart thy picture's sight would bar,

My heart, mine eye the freedom of that right.

My heart doth plead that thou in him dost lie,

A closet never pierced with crystal eyes.

But the defendant doth that plea deny,

And says in him thy fair appearance lies.

To 'cide this title is impanelled

A quest of thoughts, all tenants to the heart,

And by their verdict is determined

The clear eye's moiety, and the dear heart's part.

As thus, mine eye's due is thy outward part,

And my heart's right, thy inward love of heart.

四六

我的眼和我的心在作殊死战，
怎样去把你姣好的容貌分赃；
眼儿要把心和你的形象隔断，
心儿又不甘愿把这权利相让。

心儿声称你在它的深处潜隐，
从没有明眸闯得进它的宝箱；
被告却把这申辩坚决地否认，
说是你的倩影在它里面珍藏。

为解决这悬案就不得不邀请
我心里所有的住户——思想——协商；
它们的共同的判词终于决定
明眸和亲挚的心应得的分量

如下：你的仪表属于我的眼睛，
而我的心占有你心里的爱情。

Sonnet 47

Betwixt mine eye and heart a league is took,

And each doth good turns now unto the other,

When that mine eye is famished for a look,

Or heart in love with sighs himself doth smother,

With my love's picture then my eye doth feast,

And to the painted banquet bids my heart;

Another time mine eye is my heart's guest,

And in his thoughts of love doth share a part.

So, either by thy picture or my love,

Thyself away, art present still with me,

For thou not farther than my thoughts canst move,

And I am still with them, and they with thee.

Or if they sleep, thy picture in my sight

Awakes my heart, to heart's and eye's delight.

四七

现在我的眼和心缔结了同盟，
为的是互相帮忙和互相救济：
当眼儿渴望要一见你的尊容，
或痴情的心快要给叹气窒息，

眼儿就把你的画像大摆筵桌，
邀请心去参加这图画的盛宴；
有时候眼睛又是心的座上客，
去把它缱绻的情思平均分沾。

这样，或靠你的像或我的依恋，
你本人虽远离还是和我在一起；
你不能比我的情思走得更远，
我老跟着它们，它们又跟着你。

或者，它们倘睡着，我眼中的像
就把心唤醒，使心和眼都舒畅。

Sonnet 48

How careful was I when I took my way,

Each trifle under truest bars to thrust,

That to my use it might unused stay

From hands of falsehood, in sure wards of trust!

But thou, to whom my jewels trifles are,

Most worthy comfort, now my greatest grief,

Thou best of dearest, and mine only care,

Art left the prey of every vulgar thief.

Thee have I not locked up in any chest,

Save where thou art not, though I feel thou art,

Within the gentle closure of my breast,

From whence at pleasure thou mayst come and part;

And even thence thou wilt be stol'n I fear,

For truth proves thievish for a prize so dear.

四八

我是多么小心，在未上路之前，
为了留以备用，把琐碎的事物
——锁在箱子里，使得到保险，
不致被一些奸诈的手所亵渎！

但你，比起你来珠宝也成废品，
你，我最亲最好和唯一的牵挂，
无上的慰安（现在是最大的伤心）
却留下来让每个扒手任意拿。

我没有把你锁进任何保险箱，
除了你不在的地方，而我觉得
你在，那就是我的温暖的心房，
从那里你可以随便进进出出；

就是在那里我还怕你被偷走：
看见这样珍宝，忠诚也变扒手。

Sonnet 49

Against that time, if ever that time come,

When I shall see thee frown on my defects,

When as thy love hath cast his utmost sum,

Called to that audit by advised respects;

Against that time when thou shalt strangely pass,

And scarcely greet me with that sun thine eye,

When love, converted from the thing it was,

Shall reasons find of settled gravity;

Against that time do I ensconce me here,

Within the knowledge of mine own desert,

And this my hand, against myself uprear,

To guard the lawful reasons on thy part.

To leave poor me, thou hast the strength of laws,

Since why to love, I can allege no cause.

四九

为抵抗那一天，要是终有那一天，
当我看见你对我的缺点蹙额，
当你的爱已花完最后一文钱，
被周详的顾虑催去清算账目；

为抵抗那一天，当你像生客走过，
不用那太阳——你眼睛——向我致候，
当爱情，已改变了面目，要搜罗
种种必须决绝的庄重的理由；

为抵抗那一天我就躲在这里，
在对自己的恰当评价内安身，
并且高举我这只手当众宣誓，
为你的种种合法的理由保证：

抛弃可怜的我，你有法律保障，
既然为什么爱，我无理由可讲。

Sonnet 50

How heavy do I journey on the way,

When what I seek, my weary travel's end,

Doth teach that ease and that repose to say

'Thus far the miles are measured from thy friend!'

The beast that bears me, tired with my woe,

Plods dully on, to bear that weight in me,

As if by some instinct the wretch did know

His rider loved not speed being made from thee.

The bloody spur cannot provoke him on,

That sometimes anger thrusts into his hide,

Which heavily he answers with a groan,

More sharp to me than spurring to his side;

For that same groan doth put this in my mind,

My grief lies onward and my joy behind.

五○

多么沉重地我在旅途上跋涉，
当我的目的地（我倦旅的终点）
唆使安逸和休憩这样对我说：
　"你又离开了你的朋友那么远！"

那驮我的畜牲，经不起我的忧厄，
驮着我心里的重负慢慢地走，
仿佛这畜牲凭某种本能晓得
它主人不爱快，因为离你远游。

有时恼怒用那血淋淋的靴钉
猛刺它的皮，也不能把它催促；
它只是沉重地报以一声呻吟，
对于我，比刺它的靴钉还要残酷；

因为这呻吟使我省悟和熟筹：
我的忧愁在前面，快乐在后头。

Sonnet 51

Thus can my love excuse the slow offence

Of my dull bearer, when from thee I speed,

From where thou art, why should I haste me thence?

Till I return, of posting is no need.

O! what excuse will my poor beast then find,

When swift extremity can seem but slow?

Then should I spur, though mounted on the wind,

In winged speed no motion shall I know.

Then can no horse with my desire keep pace,

Therefore desire, of perfect'st love being made,

Shall neigh, no dull flesh, in his fiery race,

But love, for love, thus shall excuse my jade,

Since from thee going, he went wilful-slow,

Towards thee I'll run, and give him leave to go.

五一

这样，我的爱就可原谅那笨兽
（当我离开你），不嫌它走得太慢。
从你所在地我何必匆匆跑走？
除非是归来，绝对不用把路赶。

那时可怜的畜牲怎会得宽容，
当极端的迅速还要显得迟钝？
那时我就要猛刺，纵使在御风，
如飞的速度我只觉得是停顿。

那时就没有马能和欲望齐驱；
因此，欲望，由最理想的爱构成，
就引颈长嘶，当它火似地飞驰；
但爱，为了爱，将这样饶恕那畜牲：

既然别你的时候它有意慢走，
归途我就下来跑，让它得自由。

Sonnet 52

So am I as the rich whose blessed key,

Can bring him to his sweet up-locked treasure,

The which he will not every hour survey,

For blunting the fine point of seldom pleasure.

Therefore are feasts so solemn and so rare,

Since seldom coming in that long year set,

Like stones of worth they thinly placed are,

Or captain jewels in the carcanet.

So is the time that keeps you as my chest

Or as the wardrobe which the robe doth hide,

To make some special instant special-blest,

By new unfolding his imprisoned pride.

Blessed are you whose worthiness gives scope,

Being had to triumph, being lacked to hope.

五二

我像那富翁，他那幸运的钥匙
能把他带到他的心爱的宝藏，
可是他并不愿时常把它启视，
以免磨钝那难得的锐利的快感。

所以过节是那么庄严和希有，
因为在一年中仅疏疏地来临，
就像宝石在首饰上稀稀嵌就，
或大颗的珍珠在璎珞上晶莹。

同样，那保存你的时光就好像
我的宝箱，或装着华服的衣橱，
以便偶一重展那被囚的宝光，
使一些幸福的良辰分外幸福。

你真运气，你的美德能够使人
有你，喜洋洋，你不在，不胜憧憬。

Sonnet 53

What is your substance, whereof are you made,

That millions of strange shadows on you tend?

Since every one, hath every one, one shade,

And you but one, can every shadow lend.

Describe Adonis, and the counterfeit

Is poorly imitated after you;

On Helen's cheek all art of beauty set,

And you in Grecian tires are painted new.

Speak of the spring, and foison of the year,

The one doth shadow of your beauty show,

The other as your bounty doth appear,

And you in every blessed shape we know.

In all external grace you have some part,

But you like none, none you, for constant heart.

五三

你的本质是什么，用什么造成，
使得万千个倩影都追随着你？
每人都只有一个，每人，一个影；
你一人，却能幻作千万个影子。

试为阿都尼①写生，他的画像
不过是模仿你的拙劣的赝品；
尽量把美容术施在海伦颊上，
便是你披上希腊妆的新的真身。

一提起春的明媚和秋的丰饶，
一个把你的绰约的倩影显示，
另一个却是你的慷慨的写照；
一切天生的俊秀都蕴含着你。

一切外界的妩媚都有你的份，
但谁都没有你那颗坚贞的心。

---

① 现译阿多尼斯。希腊神话人物，爱神维纳斯的情人，以俊美著称，后世成为"美少年、美男子"的代名词。

Sonnet 54

O! how much more doth beauty beauteous seem
By that sweet ornament which truth doth give.
The rose looks fair, but fairer we it deem
For that sweet odour, which doth in it live.

The canker blooms have full as deep a dye
As the perfumed tincture of the roses,
Hang on such thorns, and play as wantonly,
When summer's breath their masked buds discloses;

But, for their virtue only is their show,
They live unwooed, and unrespected fade,
Die to themselves. Sweet roses do not so,
Of their sweet deaths, are sweetest odours made:

And so of you, beauteous and lovely youth,
When that shall vade, by verse distills your truth.

五四

哦，美看起来要更美得多少倍，
若再有真加给它温馨的装潢！
玫瑰花很美，但我们觉得它更美，
因为它吐出一缕甜蜜的芳香。

野蔷薇的姿色也是同样旖旎，
比起玫瑰的芳馥四溢的姣颜，
同挂在树上，同样会搔首弄姿，
当夏天呼息使它的嫩蕊轻展。

但它们唯一的美德只在色相，
开时无人眷恋，萎谢也无人理，
寂寞地死去。香的玫瑰却两样，
她那温馨的死可以酿成香液。

你也如此，美丽而可爱的青春，
当韶华凋谢，诗提取你的纯精。

Sonnet 55

Not marble, nor the gilded monuments

Of princes, shall outlive this powerful rhyme;

But you shall shine more bright in these contents

Than unswept stone, besmeared with sluttish time.

When wasteful war shall statues overturn,

And broils root out the work of masonry,

Nor Mars his sword, nor war's quick fire shall burn

The living record of your memory.

'Gainst death, and all-oblivious enmity

Shall you pace forth; your praise shall still find room

Even in the eyes of all posterity

That wear this world out to the ending doom.

So, till the judgment that yourself arise,

You live in this, and dwell in lovers' eyes.

五五

没有云石或王公们金的墓碑
能够和我这些强劲的诗比寿；
你将永远闪耀于这些诗篇里，
远胜过那被时光涂脏的石头。

当着残暴的战争把铜像推翻，
或内讧把城池荡成一片废墟，
无论战神的剑或战争的烈焰
都毁不掉你的遗芳的活历史。

突破死亡和湮没一切的仇恨，
你将昂然站起来：对你的赞美
将在万世万代的眼睛里彪炳，
直到这世界消耗完了的末日。

这样，直到最后审判把你唤醒，
你长在诗里和情人眼里辉映。

Sonnet 56

Sweet love, renew thy force, be it not said
Thy edge should blunter be than appetite,
Which but to-day by feeding is allayed,
Tomorrow sharpened in his former might.

So, love, be thou, although to-day thou fill
Thy hungry eyes, even till they wink with fulness,
Tomorrow see again, and do not kill
The spirit of love, with a perpetual dulness.

Let this sad interim like the ocean be
Which parts the shore, where two contracted new
Come daily to the banks, that when they see
Return of love, more blest may be the view.

Or call it winter, which being full of care,
Makes summer's welcome, thrice more wished, more rare.

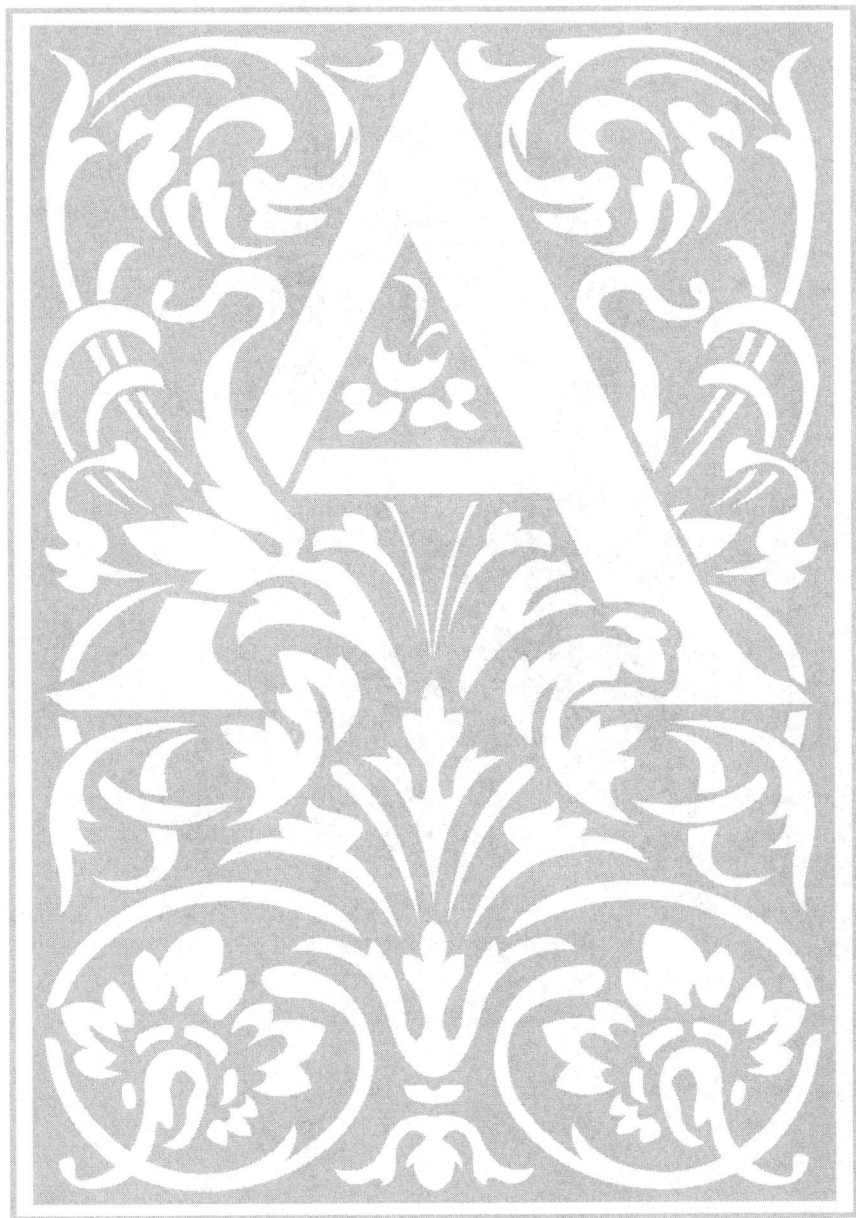

五六

温柔的爱，恢复你的劲：别被说
你的刀锋赶不上食欲那样快，
食欲只今天饱餐后暂觉满足，
到明天又照旧一样饕餐起来。

愿你，爱呵，也一样：你那双饿眼
尽管今天已饱看到腻得直眨，
明天还得看，别让长期的瘫痪
把那爱情的精灵活生生窒煞。

让这凄凉的间歇恰像那隔断
两岸的海洋，那里一对情侣
每天到岸边相会，当他们看见
爱的来归，心里感到加倍欢愉。

否则，唤它做冬天，充满了忧悒，
使夏至三倍受欢迎，三倍希奇。

Sonnet 57

Being your slave what should I do but tend

Upon the hours, and times of your desire?

I have no precious time at all to spend;

Nor services to do till you require.

Nor dare I chide the world-without-end hour,

Whilst I, my sovereign, watch the clock for you,

Nor think the bitterness of absence sour,

When you have bid your servant once adieu;

Nor dare I question with my jealous thought,

Where you may be, or your affairs suppose,

But, like a sad slave, stay and think of nought

Save, where you are, how happy you make those.

So true a fool is love, that in your will,

Though you do any thing, he thinks no ill.

五七

既然是你奴隶，我有什么可做，
除了时时刻刻伺候你的心愿？
我毫无宝贵的时间可消磨，
也无事可做，直到你有所驱遣。

我不敢骂那绵绵无尽的时刻，
当我为你，主人，把时辰来看守；
也不敢埋怨别离是多么残酷，
在你已经把你的仆人辞退后；

也不敢用妒忌的念头去探索
你究竟在哪里，或者为什么忙碌，
只是，像个可怜的奴隶，呆想着
你所在的地方，人们会多幸福。

爱这呆子是那么无救药的呆，
凭你为所欲为，他都不觉得坏。

Sonnet 58

That god forbid, that made me first your slave,

I should in thought control your times of pleasure,

Or at your hand the account of hours to crave,

Being your vassal, bound to stay your leisure!

O! let me suffer, being at your beck,

The imprisoned absence of your liberty;

And patience, tame to sufferance, bide each check,

Without accusing you of injury.

Be where you list, your charter is so strong

That you yourself may privilage your time

To what you will; to you it doth belong

Yourself to pardon of self-doing crime.

I am to wait, though waiting so be hell,

Not blame your pleasure be it ill or well.

五八

那使我做你奴隶的神不容我，
如果我要管制你行乐的时光，
或者清算你怎样把日子消磨，
既然是奴隶，就得听从你放浪。

让我忍受，既然什么都得依你，
你那自由的离弃（于我是监牢）；
让忍耐，惯了，接受每一次申斥，
绝不会埋怨你对我损害分毫。

无论你高兴到哪里，你那契约
那么有效，你自有绝对的主权
去支配你的时间；你犯的罪过
你也有主权随意把自己赦免。

我只能等待，虽然等待是地狱，
不责备你行乐，任它是善或恶。

Sonnet 59

If there be nothing new, but that which is

Hath been before, how are our brains beguiled,

Which labouring for invention bear amis

The second burthen of a former child!

O that record could with a backward look,

Even of five hundred courses of the sun,

Show me your image in some antique book,

Since mind at first in character was done.

That I might see what the old world could say

To this composed wonder of your frame;

Whether we are mended, or whether better they,

Or whether revolution be the same.

O sure I am the wits of former days,

To subjects worse have given admiring praise.

五九

如果天下无新事，现在的种种
从前都有过，我们的头脑多上当，
当它苦心要创造，却怀孕成功
一个前代有过的婴孩的重担！

哦，但愿历史能用回溯的眼光
（纵使太阳已经运行了五百周），
在古书里对我显示你的肖像，
自从心灵第一次写成了句读！——

让我晓得古人曾经怎样说法，
关于你那雍容的体态的神奇；
是我们高明，还是他们优越，
或者所谓演变其实并无二致。

哦，我敢肯定，不少才子在前代
曾经赞扬过远不如你的题材。

Sonnet 60

Like as the waves make towards the pebbled shore,

So do our minutes hasten to their end;

Each changing place with that which goes before,

In sequent toil all forwards do contend.

Nativity, once in the main of light,

Crawls to maturity, wherewith being crowned,

Crooked eclipses 'gainst his glory fight,

And Time that gave, doth now his gift confound.

Time doth transfix the flourish set on youth

And delves the parallels in beauty's brow,

Feeds on the rarities of nature's truth,

And nothing stands but for his scythe to mow.

And yet to times in hope, my verse shall stand

Praising thy worth, despite his cruel hand.

六〇

像波浪滔滔不息地滚向沙滩：
我们的光阴息息奔赴着终点；
后浪和前浪不断地循环替换，
前推后拥，一个个在奋勇争先。

生辰，一度涌现于光明的金海，
爬行到壮年，然后，既登上极顶，
凶冥的日蚀便遮没它的光彩，
时光又撕毁了它从前的赠品。

时光戳破了青春颊上的光艳，
在美的前额挖下深陷的战壕，
自然的至珍都被它肆意狂啖，
一切挺立的都难逃它的镰刀。

可是我的诗未来将屹立千古，
歌颂你的美德，不管它多残酷！

Sonnet 61

Is it thy will, thy image should keep open

My heavy eyelids to the weary night?

Dost thou desire my slumbers should be broken,

While shadows like to thee do mock my sight?

Is it thy spirit that thou send'st from thee

So far from home into my deeds to pry,

To find out shames and idle hours in me,

The scope and tenure of thy jealousy?

O, no! thy love, though much, is not so great,

It is my love that keeps mine eye awake,

Mine own true love that doth my rest defeat,

To play the watchman ever for thy sake.

For thee watch I, whilst thou dost wake elsewhere,

From me far off, with others all too near.

六一

你是否故意用影子使我垂垂
欲闭的眼睛睁向厌厌的长夜？
你是否要我辗转反侧不成寐，
用你的影子来玩弄我的视野？

那可是从你那里派来的灵魂
远离了家园，来刺探我的行为，
来找我的荒废和耻辱的时辰，
和执行你的妒忌的职权和范围？

不呀！你的爱，虽多，并不那么大；
是我的爱使我张开我的眼睛，
是我的真情把我的睡眠打垮，
为你的缘故一夜守候到天明！

我为你守夜，而你在别处清醒，
远远背着我，和别人却太靠近。

Sonnet 62

Sin of self-love possesseth all mine eye,

And all my soul, and all my every part;

And for this sin there is no remedy,

It is so grounded inward in my heart.

Methinks no face so gracious is as mine,

No shape so true, no truth of such account,

And for myself mine own worth do define,

As I all other in all worths surmount.

But when my glass shows me myself indeed,

Beated and chopt with tanned antiquity,

Mine own self-love quite contrary I read;

Self so self-loving were iniquity.

'Tis thee (myself) that for myself I praise,

Painting my age with beauty of thy days.

六二

自爱这罪恶占据着我的眼睛,
我整个的灵魂和我身体各部,
而对这罪恶什么药石都无灵,
在我心内扎根扎得那么深固。

我相信我自己的眉目最秀丽,
态度最率真,胸怀又那么俊伟;
我的优点对我这样估计自己:
不管哪一方面我都出类拔萃。

但当我的镜子照出我的真相,
全被那焦黑的老年剁得稀烂,
我对于自爱又有相反的感想:
这样溺爱着自己实在是罪愆。

我歌颂自己就等于把你歌颂,
用你的青春来粉刷我的隆冬。

Sonnet 63

Against my love shall be, as I am now,

With Time's injurious hand crushed and o'er-worn;

When hours have drained his blood and filled his brow

With lines and wrinkles, when his youthful morn

Hath travelled on to age's steepy night,

And all those beauties whereof now he's king

Are vanishing, or vanished out of sight,

Stealing away the treasure of his spring;

For such a time do I now fortify

Against confounding age's cruel knife,

That he shall never cut from memory

My sweet love's beauty, though my lover's life.

His beauty shall in these black lines be seen,

And they shall live, and he in them still green.

六三

像我现在一样，我爱人将不免
被时光的毒手所粉碎和消耗，
当时辰吮干他的血，使他的脸
布满了皱纹；当他韶年的清朝

已经爬到暮年的巉岩的黑夜，
使他所占领的一切风流逸韵
都渐渐消灭或已经全部消灭，
偷走了他的春天所有的至珍；

为那时候我现在就厉兵秣马
去抵抗凶暴时光的残酷利刃，
使他无法把我爱的芳菲抹煞，
虽则他能够砍断我爱的生命。

他的丰韵将在这些诗里现形，
墨迹长在，而他也将万古长青。

Sonnet 64

When I have seen by Time's fell hand defaced

The rich-proud cost of outworn buried age,

When sometime lofty towers I see down-rased,

And brass eternal slave to mortal rage.

When I have seen the hungry ocean gain

Advantage on the kingdom of the shore,

And the firm soil win of the watery main,

Increasing store with loss, and loss with store.

When I have seen such interchange of State,

Or state itself confounded, to decay,

Ruin hath taught me thus to ruminate

That Time will come and take my love away.

This thought is as a death which cannot choose

But weep to have, that which it fears to lose.

六四

当我眼见前代的富丽和豪华
被时光的手毫不留情地磨灭；
当巍峨的塔我眼见沦为碎瓦，
连不朽的铜也不免一场浩劫；

当我眼见那欲壑难填的大海
一步一步把岸上的疆土侵蚀，
汪洋的水又渐渐被陆地覆盖，
失既变成了得，得又变成了失；

当我看见这一切扰攘和废兴，
或者连废兴一旦也化为乌有；
毁灭便教我再三这样地反省：
时光终要跑来把我的爱带走。

哦，多么致命的思想！它只能够
哭着去把那刻刻怕失去的占有。

Sonnet 65

Since brass, nor stone, nor earth, nor boundless sea,

But sad mortality o'ersways their power,

How with this rage shall beauty hold a plea,

Whose action is no stronger than a flower?

O, how shall summer's honey breath hold out

Against the wrackful siege of batt'ring days,

When rocks impregnable are not so stout,

Nor gates of steel so strong, but time decays?

O fearful meditation! where alack,

Shall Time's best jewel from Time's chest lie hid?

Or what strong hand can hold his swift foot back?

Or who his spoil of beauty can forbid?

O, none, unless this miracle have might,

That in black ink my love may still shine bright.

六五

既然铜、石、或大地、或无边的海，
没有不屈服于那阴惨的无常，
美，她的活力比一朵花还柔脆，
怎能和他那肃杀的严威抵抗？

哦，夏天温馨的呼吸怎能支持
残暴的日子刻刻猛烈的轰炸，
当岩石，无论多么么险固，或钢扉，
无论多坚强，都要被时光熔化？

哦，骇人的思想！时光的珍饰，
唉，怎能够不被收进时光的宝箱？
什么劲手能挽他的捷足回来，
或者谁能禁止他把美丽夺抢？

哦，没有谁，除非这奇迹有力量：
我的爱在翰墨里永久放光芒。

Sonnet 66

Tired with all these, for restful death I cry,

As to behold desert a beggar born,

And needy nothing trimmed in jollity,

And purest faith unhappily forsworn,

And gilded honour shamefully misplaced,

And maiden virtue rudely strumpeted,

And right perfection wrongfully disgraced,

And strength by limping sway disabled,

And art made tongue-tied by authority,

And folly doctor-like controlling skill,

And simple truth miscalled simplicity,

And captive good attending captain ill.

Tired with all these, from these would I be gone,

Save that, to die, I leave my love alone.

六六

厌了这一切，我向安息的死疾呼，
比方，眼见天才注定做叫化子，
无聊的草包打扮得衣冠楚楚，
纯洁的信义不幸而被人背弃，

金冠可耻地戴在行尸的头上，
处女的贞操遭受暴徒的玷辱，
严肃的正义被人非法地诟让，
壮士被当权的跛子弄成残缺，

愚蠢摆起博士架子驾驭才能，
艺术被官府统治得结舌箝口，
淳朴的真诚被人瞎称为愚笨，
囚徒"善"不得不把统帅"恶"伺候：

厌了这一切，我要离开人寰，
但，我一死，我的爱人便孤单。

Sonnet 67

Ah! wherefore with infection should he live,

And with his presence grace impiety,

That sin by him advantage should achieve

And lace itself with his society?

Why should false painting imitate his cheek

And steal dead seeming of his living hue?

Why should poor beauty indirectly seek

Roses of shadow, since his rose is true?

Why should he live, now nature bankrupt is,

Beggared of blood to blush through lively veins,

For she hath no exchequer now but his,

And, proud of many, lives upon his gains?

O, him she stores, to show what wealth she had

In days long since, before these last so bad.

六七

唉，我的爱为什么要和臭腐同居，
把他的绰约的丰姿让人亵渎，
以至罪恶得以和他结成伴侣，
涂上纯洁的外表来眩耀耳目？

骗人的脂粉为什么要替他写真，
从他的奕奕神采偷取死形似？
为什么，既然他是玫瑰花的真身，
可怜的美还要找玫瑰的影子？

为什么他得活着，当造化破了产，
缺乏鲜血去灌注淡红的脉络？
因为造化现在只有他作富源，
自夸富有，却靠他的利润过活。

哦，她珍藏他，为使荒歉的今天
认识从前曾有过怎样的丰年。

Sonnet 68

Thus is his cheek the map of days outworn,

When beauty lived and died as flowers do now,

Before these bastard signs of fair were born,

Or durst inhabit on a living brow;

Before the golden tresses of the dead,

The right of sepulchres, were shorn away,

To live a second life on second head,

Ere beauty's dead fleece made another gay.

In him those holy antique hours are seen,

Without all ornament, itself and true,

Making no summer of another's green,

Robbing no old to dress his beauty new;

And him as for a map doth Nature store,

To show false Art what beauty was of yore.

六八

这样，他的朱颜是古代的图志，
那时美开了又谢像今天花一样，
那时冒牌的艳色还未曾出世，
或未敢公然高据活人的额上，

那时死者的美发，坟墓的财产，
还未被偷剪下来，去活第二回
在第二个头上①；那时美的死金鬈
还未被用来使别人显得华贵。

这圣洁的古代在他身上呈现，
赤裸裸的真容，毫无一点铅华，
不用别人的青翠做他的夏天，
不掠取旧脂粉妆饰他的鲜花。

就这样造化把他当图志珍藏，
让假艺术赏识古代美的真相。

---

① 当时制造假发的人常常买死人的头发作原料。

Sonnet 69

Those parts of thee that the world's eye doth view
Want nothing that the thought of hearts can mend.
All tongues, the voice of souls, give thee that due,
Uttering bare truth, even so as foes commend.

Thy outward thus with outward praise is crowned,
But those same tongues that give thee so thine own
In other accents do this praise confound
By seeing farther than the eye hath shown.

They look into the beauty of thy mind,
And that, in guess, they measure by thy deeds,
Then, churls, their thoughts, although their eyes were kind,
To thy fair flower add the rank smell of weeds.

But why thy odour matcheth not thy show,
The soil is this, that thou dost common grow.

六九

你那众目共睹的无瑕的芳容，
谁的心思都不能再加以增改；
众口，灵魂的声音，都一致赞同：
赤的真理，连仇人也无法掩盖。

这样，表面的赞扬载满你仪表；
但同一声音，既致应有的崇敬，
便另换口吻去把这赞扬勾销，
当心灵看到眼看不到的内心。

它们向你那灵魂的美的海洋
用你的操行作测量器去探究，
于是吝啬的思想，眼睛虽大方，
便加给你的鲜花以野草的恶臭：

为什么你的香味赶不上外观？
土壤是这样，你自然长得平凡。

Sonnet 70

That thou art blamed shall not be thy defect,

For slander's mark was ever yet the fair,

The ornament of beauty is suspect,

A crow that flies in heaven's sweetest air.

So thou be good, slander doth but approve

Thy worth the greater, being wooed of time;

For canker vice the sweetest buds doth love,

And thou present'st a pure unstained prime.

Thou hast passed by the ambush of young days,

Either not assailed, or victor being charged;

Yet this thy praise cannot be so thy praise,

To tie up envy, evermore enlarged.

If some suspect of ill masked not thy show,

Then thou alone kingdoms of hearts shouldst owe.

七〇

你受人指摘，并不是你的瑕疵，
因为美丽永远是诽谤的对象；
美丽的无上的装饰就是猜疑，
像乌鸦在最晴朗的天空飞翔。

所以，检点些，谗言只能更恭维
你的美德，既然时光对你钟情；
因为恶蛆最爱那甜蜜的嫩蕊，
而你的正是纯洁无瑕的初春。

你已经越过年轻日子的埋伏，
或未遭遇袭击，或已克服敌手；
可是，对你这样的赞美并不足
堵住那不断扩大的嫉妒的口。

若没有猜疑把你的清光遮掩，
多少个心灵的王国将归你独占。

Sonnet 71

No longer mourn for me when I am dead

Than you shall hear the surly sullen bell

Give warning to the world that I am fled

From this vile world, with vilest worms to dwell.

Nay, if you read this line, remember not

The hand that writ it, for I love you so,

That I in your sweet thoughts would be forgot

If thinking on me then should make you woe.

O, if , I say, you look upon this verse

When I perhaps compounded am with clay,

Do not so much as my poor name rehearse.

But let your love even with my life decay,

Lest the wise world should look into your moan,

And mock you with me after I am gone.

七一

我死去的时候别再为我悲哀，
当你听见那沉重凄惨的葬钟
普告给全世界说我已经离开
这龌龊世界去伴最龌龊的虫。

不呀，当你读到这诗，别再记起
那写它的手；因为我爱到这样，
宁愿被遗忘在你甜蜜的心里，
如果想起我会使你不胜哀伤。

如果呀，我说，如果你看见这诗，
那时候或许我已经化作泥土，
连我这可怜的名字也别提起。
但愿你的爱与我的生命同腐，

免得这聪明世界猜透你的心，
在我死去后把你也当作笑柄。

Sonnet 72

O! lest the world should task you to recite

What merit lived in me that you should love

After my death, dear love, forget me quite,

For you in me can nothing worthy prove.

Unless you would devise some virtuous lie,

To do more for me than mine own desert,

And hang more praise upon deceased I

Than niggard truth would willingly impart.

O! lest your true love may seem false in this

That you for love speak well of me untrue,

My name be buried where my body is,

And live no more to shame nor me, nor you.

For I am shamed by that which I bring forth,

And so should you, to love things nothing worth.

七二

哦，免得这世界要强逼你自招
我有什么好处，使你在我死后
依旧爱我，爱人呀，把我全忘掉，
因外我一点值得提的都没有；

除非你捏造出一些美丽的谎，
过分为我吹嘘我应有的价值，
把瞑目长眠的我阿谀和夸奖，
远超过鄙吝的事实所愿昭示。

哦，怕你的真爱因此显得虚伪，
怕你为爱的缘故替我说假话，
愿我的名字永远和肉体同埋，
免得活下去把你和我都羞煞。

因为我可怜的作品使我羞惭，
而你爱不值得爱的，也该愧赧。

Sonnet 73

That time of year thou mayst in me behold
When yellow leaves, or none, or few do hang
Upon those boughs which shake against the cold,
Bare ruined choirs, where late the sweet birds sang.

In me thou seest the twilight of such day
As after sunset fadeth in the west,
Which by and by black night doth take away,
Death's second self, that seals up all in rest.

In me thou seest the glowing of such fire
That on the ashes of his youth doth lie,
As the death-bed whereon it must expire
Consumed with that which it was nourished by.

This thou perceiv'st, which makes thy love more strong,
To love that well which thou must leave ere long.

七三

在我身上你或许会看见秋天，
当黄叶，或尽脱，或只三三两两
挂在瑟缩的枯枝上索索抖颤——
荒废的歌坛，那里百鸟曾合唱。

在我身上你或许会看见暮霭，
它在日落后向西方徐徐消退。
黑夜，死的化身，渐渐把它赶开，
严静的安息笼住纷纭的万类。

在我身上你或许会看见余烬，
它在青春的寒灰里奄奄一息，
在惨淡灵床上早晚总要断魂，
给那滋养过它的烈焰所销毁。

看见了这些，你的爱就会加强，
因为他转瞬要辞你溘然长往。

Sonnet 74

But be contented when that fell arrest

Without all bail shall carry me away,

My life hath in this line some interest,

Which for memorial still with thee shall stay.

When thou reviewest this, thou dost review

The very part was consecrate to thee,

The earth can have but earth, which is his due,

My spirit is thine, the better part of me.

So then thou hast but lost the dregs of life,

The prey of worms, my body being dead,

The coward conquest of a wretch's knife,

Too base of thee to be remembered.

The worth of that, is that which it contains,

And that is this, and this with thee remains.

七四

但是放心吧：当那无情的拘票
终于丝毫不宽假地把我带走，
我的生命在诗里将依然长保，
永生的纪念品，永久和你相守。

当你重读这些诗，就等于重读
我献给你的至纯无二的生命。
尘土只能有它的份，那就是尘土；
灵魂却属你，这才是我的真身。

所以你不过失掉生命的糟粕
（当我肉体死后），恶蛆们的食饵，
无赖的刀下一个怯懦的俘获，
太卑贱的秽物，不配被你记忆。

它唯一的价值就在它的内蕴，
那就是这诗：这诗将和它长存。

Sonnet 75

So are you to my thoughts as food to life,

Or as sweet-seasoned showers are to the ground;

And for the peace of you I hold such strife

As 'twixt a miser and his wealth is found.

Now proud as an enjoyer, and anon

Doubting the filching age will steal his treasure,

Now counting best to be with you alone,

Then bettered that the world may see my pleasure;

Sometime all full with feasting on your sight,

And by and by clean starved for a look,

Possessing or pursuing no delight

Save what is had, or must from you be took.

Thus do I pine and surfeit day by day,

Or gluttoning on all, or all away.

七五

我的心需要你，像生命需要食粮，
或者像大地需要及时的甘霖；
为你的安宁我内心那么凄惶，
就像贪夫和他的财富作斗争。

他，有时自夸财主，然后又顾虑
这惯窃的时代会偷他的财宝；
我，有时觉得最好独自伴着你，
忽然又觉得该把你当众夸耀。

有时饱餐秀色后腻到化不开，
渐渐地又饿得慌要瞟你一眼；
既不占有也不追求别的欢快，
除掉那你已施或要施的恩典。

这样，我整天垂涎或整天不消化，
我狼吞虎咽，或一点也咽不下。

Sonnet 76

Why is my verse so barren of new pride,

So far from variation or quick change?

Why with the time do I not glance aside

To new-found methods, and to compounds strange?

Why write I still all one, ever the same,

And keep invention in a noted weed,

That every word doth almost tell my name,

Showing their birth, and where they did proceed?

O! know sweet love I always write of you,

And you and love are still my argument;

So all my best is dressing old words new,

Spending again what is already spent:

For as the sun is daily new and old,

So is my love still telling what is told.

七六

为什么我的诗那么缺新光彩，
赶不上现代善变多姿的风尚？
为什么我不学时人旁征博采
那竞奇斗艳，穷妍极巧的新腔？

为什么我写的始终别无二致，
寓情思旨趣于一些老调陈言，
几乎每一句都说出我的名字，
透露它们的身世，它们的来源？

哦，须知道，我爱呵，我只把你描，
你和爱情就是我唯一的主题；
推陈出新是我的无上的诀窍，
我把开支过的，不断重新开支。

因为，正如太阳天天新天天旧，
我的爱把说过的事絮絮不休。

Sonnet 77

Thy glass will show thee how thy beauties wear,

Thy dial how thy precious minutes waste;

These vacant leaves thy mind's imprint will bear,

And of this book, this learning mayst thou taste.

The wrinkles which thy glass will truly show

Of mouthed graves will give thee memory;

Thou by thy dial's shady stealth mayst know

Time's thievish progress to eternity.

Look what thy memory cannot contain,

Commit to these waste blanks, and thou shalt find

Those children nursed, delivered from thy brain,

To take a new acquaintance of thy mind.

These offices, so oft as thou wilt look,

Shall profit thee, and much enrich thy book.

七七

镜子将告诉你朱颜怎样消逝，
日规怎样一秒秒耗去你的华年；
这白纸所要记录的你的心迹
将教你细细玩味下面的教言。

你的镜子所忠实反映的皱纹
将令你记起那张开口的坟墓；
从日规上阴影的潜移你将认清，
时光走向永劫的悄悄的脚步。

看，把记忆所不能保留的东西
交给这张白纸，在那里面你将
看见你精神的产儿受到抚育，
使你重新认识你心灵的本相。

这些日课，只要你常拿来重温，
将有利于你，并丰富你的书本。

Sonnet 78

So oft have I invoked thee for my muse,

And found such fair assistance in my verse

As every alien pen hath got my use

And under thee their poesy disperse.

Thine eyes, that taught the dumb on high to sing

And heavy ignorance aloft to fly,

Have added feathers to the learned's wing

And given grace a double majesty.

Yet be most proud of that which I compile,

Whose influence is thine, and born of thee,

In others' works thou dost but mend the style,

And arts with thy sweet graces graced be.

But thou art all my art, and dost advance

As high as learning, my rude ignorance.

七八

我常常把你当诗神向你祷告，
在诗里找到那么有力的神助，
以致凡陌生的笔都把我仿效，
在你名义下把他们的诗散布。

你的眼睛，曾教会哑巴们歌唱，
曾教会沉重的愚昧高飞上天，
又把新羽毛加给博学的翅膀，
加给温文尔雅以两重的尊严。

可是我的诗应该最使你骄傲，
它们的诞生全在你的感召下。
对别人的作品你只润饰格调，
用你的美在他们才华上添花。

但对于我，你就是我全部艺术，
把我的愚拙提到博学的高度。

Sonnet 79

Whilst I alone did call upon thy aid,

My verse alone had all thy gentle grace;

But now my gracious numbers are decayed,

And my sick muse doth give an other place.

I grant, sweet love, thy lovely argument

Deserves the travail of a worthier pen;

Yet what of thee thy poet doth invent

He robs thee of, and pays it thee again.

He lends thee virtue, and he stole that word

From thy behaviour, beauty doth he give,

And found it in thy cheek: he can afford

No praise to thee, but what in thee doth live.

Then thank him not for that which he doth say,

Since what he owes thee, thou thyself dost pay.

七九

当初我独自一个恳求你协助，
只有我的诗占有你一切妩媚；
但现在我清新的韵律既陈腐，
我的病诗神只好给别人让位。

我承认，爱呵，你这美妙的题材
值得更高明的笔的精写细描；
可是你的诗人不过向你还债，
他把夺自你的当作他的创造。

他赐你美德，美德这词他只从
你的行为偷取；他加给你秀妍，
其实从你颊上得来；他的歌颂
没有一句不是从你身上发现。

那么，请别感激他对你的称赞，
既然他只把欠你的向你偿还。

Sonnet 80

O! how I faint when I of you do write,

Knowing a better spirit doth use your name,

And in the praise thereof spends all his might,

To make me tongue-tied speaking of your fame.

But since your worth , wide as the ocean is,

The humble as the proudest sail doth bear,

My saucy bark, inferior far to his,

On your broad main doth wilfully appear.

Your shallowest help will hold me up afloat,

Whilst he upon your soundless deep doth ride,

Or, being wrecked, I am a worthless boat,

He of tall building, and of goodly pride.

Then if he thrive and I be cast away,

The worst was this, my love was my decay.

八〇

哦，我写到你的时候多么气馁，
得知有更大的天才利用你名字，
他不惜费尽力气去把你赞美，
使我箝口结舌，一提起你声誉！

但你的价值，像海洋一样无边，
不管轻舟或艨艟同样能载起，
我这莽撞的艇，尽管小得可怜，
也向你茫茫的海心大胆行驶。

你最浅的滩濑已足使我浮泛，
而他岸岸然驶向你万顷汪洋；
或者，万一覆没，我只是片轻帆，
他却是结构雄伟，气宇轩昂。

如果他安全到达，而我遭失败，
最不幸的是：毁我的是我的爱。

Sonnet 81

Or I shall live your epitaph to make,

Or you survive when I in earth am rotten,

From hence your memory death cannot take,

Although in me each part will be forgotten.

Your name from hence immortal life shall have,

Though I, once gone, to all the world must die;

The earth can yield me but a common grave,

When you entombed in men's eyes shall lie.

Your monument shall be my gentle verse,

Which eyes not yet created shall o'er-read,

And tongues to be, your being shall rehearse,

When all the breathers of this world are dead.

You still shall live, such virtue hath my pen,

Where breath most breathes, even in the mouths of men.

八一

无论我将活着为你写墓志铭，
或你未亡而我已在地下腐朽，
纵使我已被遗忘得一干二净，
死神将不能把你的忆念夺走。

你的名字将从这诗里得永生，
虽然我，一去，对人间便等于死；
大地只能够给我一座乱葬坟，
而你却将长埋在人们眼睛里。

我这些小诗便是你的纪念碑，
未来的眼睛固然要百读不厌，
未来的舌头也将要传诵不衰，
当现在呼吸的人已瞑目长眠。

这强劲的笔将使你活在生气
最蓬勃的地方，在人们的嘴里。

Sonnet 82

I grant thou wert not married to my muse,

And therefore mayst without attaint o'erlook

The dedicated words which writers use

Of their fair subject, blessing every book.

Thou art as fair in knowledge as in hue,

Finding thy worth a limit past my praise;

And therefore art enforced to seek anew

Some fresher stamp of the time-bettering days.

And do so, love; yet when they have devised,

What strained touches rhetoric can lend,

Thou truly fair, wert truly sympathized

In true plain words, by thy true-telling friend.

And their gross painting might be better used

Where cheeks need blood, in thee it is abused.

八二

我承认你并没有和我的诗神
结同心，因而可以丝毫无愧恧
去俯览那些把你作主题的诗人
对你的赞美，褒奖着每本诗集。

你的智慧和姿色都一样出众，
又发觉你的价值比我的赞美高，
因而你不得不到别处去追踪
这迈进时代的更生动的写照。

就这么办，爱呵，但当他们既已
使尽了浮夸的辞藻把你刻划，
真美的你只能由真诚的知己
用真朴的话把你真实地表达。

他们的浓脂粉只配拿去染红
贫血的脸颊；对于你却是滥用。

Sonnet 83

I never saw that you did painting need,

And therefore to your fair no painting set;

I found, or thought I found, you did exceed

That barren tender of a poet's debt;

And therefore have I slept in your report,

That you yourself, being extant, well might show

How far a modern quill doth come too short,

Speaking of worth, what worth in you doth grow.

This silence for my sin you did impute,

Which shall be most my glory being dumb;

For I impair not beauty being mute,

When others would give life, and bring a tomb.

There lives more life in one of your fair eyes

Than both your poets can in praise devise.

八三

我从不觉得你需要涂脂荡粉，
因而从不用脂粉涂你的朱颜；
我发觉，或以为发觉，你的丰韵
远超过诗人献你的无味缱绻。

因此，关于你我的歌只装打盹，
好让你自己生动地现身说法，
证明时下的文笔是多么粗笨，
想把美德，你身上的美德增华。

你把我这沉默认为我的罪行，
其实却应该是我最大的荣光；
因为我不作声于美丝毫无损，
别人想给你生命，反把你埋葬。

你的两位诗人所模拟的赞美，
远不如你一只慧眼所藏的光辉。

Sonnet 84

Who is it that says most, which can say more,

Than this rich praise, that you alone, are you?

In whose confine immured is the store

Which should example where your equal grew.

Lean penury within that pen doth dwell

That to his subject lends not some small glory;

But he that writes of you, if he can tell

That you are you, so dignifies his story.

Let him but copy what in you is writ,

Not making worse what nature made so clear,

And such a counterpart shall fame his wit,

Making his style admired every where.

You to your beauteous blessings add a curse,

Being fond on praise, which makes your praises worse.

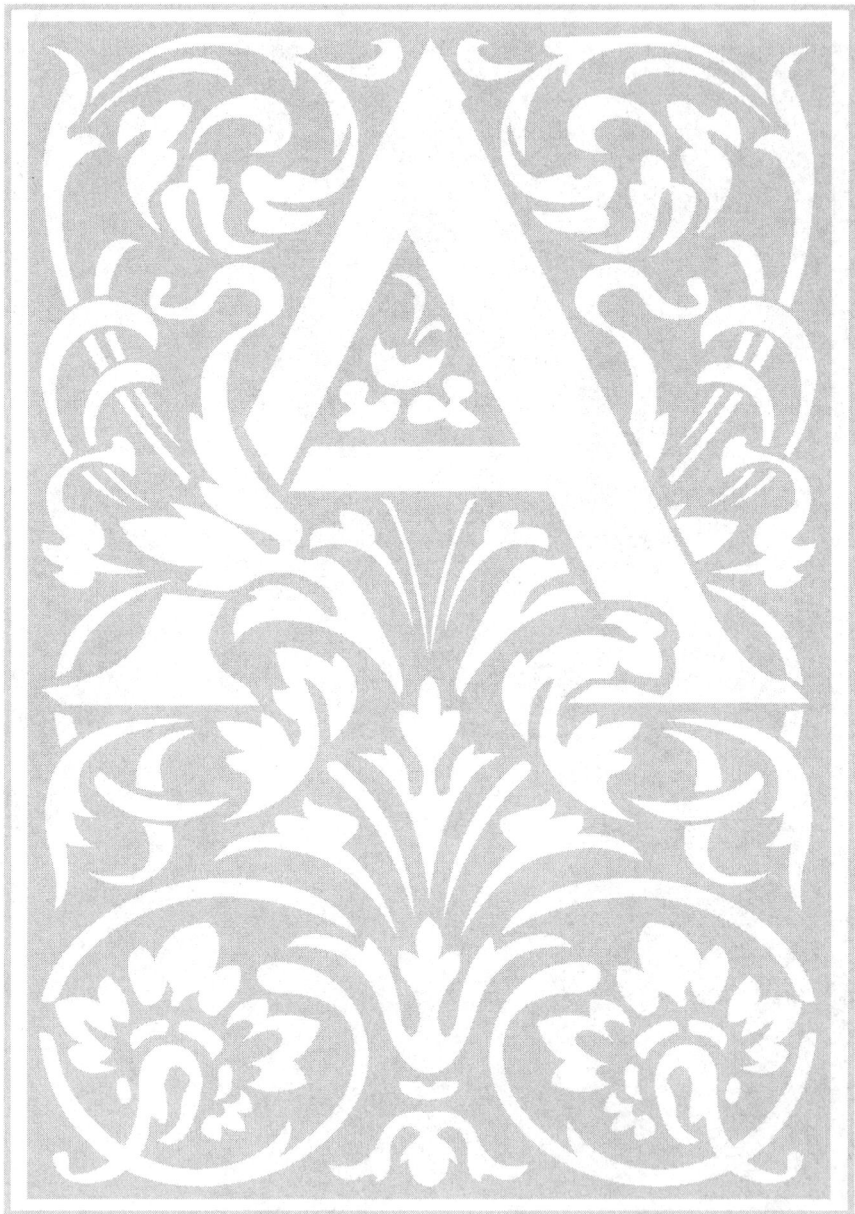

八四

谁说得最好，哪个说得更圆满，
比起这丰美的赞词："只有你是你"？
这赞词蕴藏着你的全部资产，
谁和你争妍，就必须和它比拟。

那枝文笔实在是贫瘠得可怜，
如果它不能把题材稍事增华；
但谁写到你，只要他能够表现
你就是你，他的故事已够伟大。

让他只照你原稿忠实地直抄，
别把造化的清新的素描弄坏，
这样的摹本已显出他的巧妙，
使他的风格到处受人们崇拜。

你将对你美的祝福加以咒诅：
太爱人赞美，连美也变成庸俗。

Sonnet 85

My tongue-tied muse in manners holds her still,

While comments of your praise richly compiled,

Reserve their character with golden quill,

And precious phrase by all the Muses filed.

I think good thoughts, whilst other write good words,

And like unlettered clerk still cry 'Amen'

To every hymn that able spirit affords,

In polished form of well-refined pen.

Hearing you praised, I say "'tis so, 'tis true",

And to the most of praise add something more;

But that is in my thought, whose love to you,

Though words come hindmost, holds his rank before.

Then others, for the breath of words respect,

Me for my dumb thoughts, speaking in effect.

八五

我的缄口的诗神只脉脉无语；
他们对你的美评却累牍连篇，
用金笔刻成辉煌夺目的大字，
和经过一切艺神雕琢的名言。

我满腔热情，他们却善颂善祷，
像不识字的牧师只知喊"阿门"，
去响应才子们用精炼的笔调
熔铸成的每一首赞美的歌咏。

听见人赞美你，我说，"的确，很对"，
凭他们怎样歌颂我总嫌不够；
但只在心里说，因为我对你的爱
虽拙于词令，行动却永远带头。

那么，请敬他们，为他们的虚文；
敬我，为我的哑口无言的真诚。

Sonnet 86

Was it the proud full sail of his great verse,

Bound for the prize of all too precious you,

That did my ripe thoughts in my brain inhearse,

Making their tomb the womb wherein they grew?

Was it his spirit, by spirits taught to write

Above a mortal pitch, that struck me dead?

No, neither he, nor his compeers by night

Giving him aid, my verse astonished.

He nor that affable familiar ghost

Which nightly gulls him with intelligence,

As victors of my silence cannot boast;

I was not sick of any fear from thence.

But when your countenance filled up his line,

Then lacked I matter; that enfeebled mine.

八六

是否他那雄浑的诗句，昂昂然
扬帆直驶去夺取太宝贵的你，
使我成熟的思想在脑里流产，
把孕育它们的胎盘变成墓地？

是否他的心灵，从幽灵学会写
超凡的警句，把我活生生殛毙？
不，既不是他本人，也不是黑夜
遣送给他的助手，能使我昏迷。

他，或他那个和善可亲的幽灵
（它夜夜用机智骗他），都不能自豪
是他们把我打垮，使我默不作声；
他们的威胁绝不能把我吓倒。

但当他的诗充满了你的鼓励，
我就要缺灵感；这才使我丧气。

Sonnet 87

Farewell! thou art too dear for my possessing,

And like enough thou know'st thy estimate,

The charter of thy worth gives thee releasing;

My bonds in thee are all determinate.

For how do I hold thee but by thy granting?

And for that riches where is my deserving?

The cause of this fair gift in me is wanting,

And so my patent back again is swerving.

Thyself thou gavest, thy own worth then not knowing,

Or me to whom thou gavest it, else mistaking;

So thy great gift, upon misprision growing,

Comes home again, on better judgement making.

Thus have I had thee, as a dream doth flatter,

In sleep a king, but waking no such matter.

八七

再会吧！你太宝贵了，我无法高攀；
显然你也晓得你自己的声价：
你的价值的证券够把你赎还，
我对你的债权只好全部作罢。

因为，不经你批准，我怎能占有你？
我哪有福气消受这样的珍宝？
这美惠对于我既然毫无根据，
便不得不取消我的专利执照。

你曾许了我，因为低估了自己，
不然就错识了我，你的受赐者；
因此，你这份厚礼，既出自误会，
就归还给你，经过更好的判决。

这样，我曾占有你，像一个美梦，
在梦里称王，醒来只是一场空。

Sonnet 88

When thou shalt be disposed to set me light,

And place my merit in the eye of scorn,

Upon thy side, against myself I'll fight,

And prove thee virtuous, though thou art forsworn.

With mine own weakness being best acquainted,

Upon thy part I can set down a story

Of faults concealed, wherein I am attainted;

That thou in losing me, shalt win much glory:

And I by this will be a gainer too;

For bending all my loving thoughts on thee,

The injuries that to myself I do,

Doing thee vantage, double-vantage me.

Such is my love, to thee I so belong,

That for thy right, myself will bear all wrong.

八八

当你有一天下决心瞧我不起，
用侮蔑的眼光衡量我的轻重，
我将站在你那边打击我自己，
证明你贤德，尽管你已经背盟。

对自己的弱点我既那么内行，
我将为你的利益捏造我种种
无人觉察的过失，把自己中伤，
使你抛弃了我反而得到光荣。

而我也可以借此而大有收获；
因为我全部情思那么倾向你，
我为自己所招惹的一切侮辱
既对你有利，对我就加倍有利。

我那么衷心属你，我爱到那样，
为你的美誉愿承当一切诽谤。

Sonnet 89

Say that thou didst forsake me for some fault,

And I will comment upon that offence,

Speak of my lameness, and I straight will halt,

Against thy reasons making no defence.

Thou canst not, love, disgrace me half so ill,

To set a form upon desired change,

As I'll myself disgrace; knowing thy will,

I will acquaintance strangle, and look strange;

Be absent from thy walks; and in my tongue

Thy sweet beloved name no more shall dwell,

Lest I, too much profane, should do it wrong,

And haply of our old acquaintance tell.

For thee, against myself I'll vow debate,

For I must ne'er love him whom thou dost hate.

八九

说你抛弃我是为了我的过失,
我立刻会对这冒犯加以阐说:
叫我做瘸子,我马上两脚都蹩,
对你的理由绝不作任何反驳。

为了替你的反复无常找借口,
爱呵,凭你怎样侮辱我,总比不上
我侮辱自己来得厉害;既看透
你心肠,我就要绞杀交情,假装

路人避开你;你那可爱的名字,
那么香,将永不挂在我的舌头,
生怕我,太亵渎了,会把它委屈;
万一还会把我们的旧欢泄漏。

我为你将展尽辩才反对自己,
因为你所憎恶的,我绝不爱惜。

Sonnet 90

Then hate me when thou wilt; if ever, now;

Now, while the world is bent my deeds to cross,

Join with the spite of fortune, make me bow,

And do not drop in for an after-loss.

Ah! do not, when my heart hath 'scaped this sorrow,

Come in the rearward of a conquered woe;

Give not a windy night a rainy morrow,

To linger out a purposed overthrow.

If thou wilt leave me, do not leave me last,

When other petty griefs have done their spite,

But in the onset come, so shall I taste

At first the very worst of fortune's might.

And other strains of woe, which now seem woe,

Compared with loss of thee, will not seem so.

九〇

恨我，倘若你高兴；请现在就开首；
现在，当举世都起来和我作对，
请趁势为命运助威，逼我低头，
别意外地走来作事后的摧毁。

唉，不要，当我的心已摆脱烦恼，
来为一个已克服的厄难作殿，
不要在暴风后再来一个雨朝，
把那注定的浩劫的来临拖延。

如果你要离开我，别等到最后，
当其他的烦忧已经肆尽暴虐；
请一开头就来：让我好先尝够
命运的权威应有尽有的凶恶。

于是别的苦痛，现在显得苦痛，
比起丧失你来便要无影无踪。

Sonnet 91

Some glory in their birth, some in their skill,

Some in their wealth, some in their body's force,

Some in their garments though new-fangled ill;

Some in their hawks and hounds, some in their horse.

And every humour hath his adjunct pleasure,

Wherein it finds a joy above the rest,

But these particulars are not my measure,

All these I better in one general best.

Thy love is better than high birth to me,

Richer than wealth, prouder than garments' costs,

Of more delight than hawks and horses be;

And having thee, of all men's pride I boast:

Wretched in this alone, that thou mayst take

All this away, and me most wretchcd make.

九一

有人夸耀门第，有人夸耀技巧，
有人夸耀财富，有人夸耀体力；
有人夸耀新妆，丑怪尽管时髦；
有人夸耀鹰犬，有人夸耀骏骥；

每种嗜好都各饶特殊的趣味，
每一种都各自以为其乐无穷。
可是这些癖好都不合我口胃——
我把它们融入更大的乐趣中。

你的爱对我比门第还要豪华，
比财富还要丰裕，比艳妆光彩，
它的乐趣远胜过鹰犬和骏马；
有了你，我便可以笑傲全世界。

只有这点可怜：你随时可罢免
我这一切，使我成无比的可怜。

Sonnet 92

But do thy worst to steal thyself away,

For term of life thou art assured mine,

And life no longer than thy love will stay,

For it depends upon that love of thine.

Then need I not to fear the worst of wrongs,

When in the least of them my life hath end.

I see a better state to me belongs

Than that, which on thy humour doth depend;

Thou canst not vex me with inconstant mind,

Since that my life on thy revolt doth lie.

O, what a happy title do I find,

Happy to have thy love, happy to die!

But what's so blessed-fair that fears no blot?

Thou mayst be false, and yet I know it not.

九二

但尽管你不顾一切偷偷溜走，
直到生命终点你还是属于我。
生命也不会比你的爱更长久，
因为生命只靠你的爱才能活。

因此，我就不用怕最大的灾害，
既然最小的已足置我于死地。
我瞥见一个对我更幸福的境界，
它不会随着你的爱憎而转移。

你的反复再也不能使我颓丧，
既然你一反脸我生命便完毕。
哦，我找到了多么幸福的保障：
幸福地享受你的爱，幸福地死去！

但人间哪有不怕玷污的美满？
你可以变心肠，同时对我隐瞒。

Sonnet 93

So shall I live, supposing thou art true,

Like a deceived husband; so love's face

May still seem love to me, though altered new;

Thy looks with me, thy heart in other place.

For there can live no hatred in thine eye,

Therefore in that I cannot know thy change,

In many's looks, the false heart's history

Is writ in moods, and frowns, and wrinkles strange.

But heaven in thy creation did decree

That in thy face sweet love should ever dwell;

Whate'er thy thoughts, or thy heart's workings be,

Thy looks should nothing thence, but sweetness tell.

How like Eve's apple doth thy beauty grow,

If thy sweet virtue answer not thy show.

九三

于是我将活下去，认定你忠贞，
像被骗的丈夫，于是爱的面目
对我仍旧是爱，虽则已翻了新；
眼睛尽望着我，心儿却在别处。

憎恨既无法存在于你的眼里，
我就无法看出你心肠的改变。
许多人每段假情假义的历史
都在颦眉、蹙额或气色上表现；

但上天造你的时候早已注定
柔情要永远在你的脸上逗留；
不管你的心怎样变幻无凭准，
你眼睛只能诉说旖旎和温柔。

你的妩媚会变成夏娃的苹果，
如果你的美德跟外表不配合。

Sonnet 94

They that have power to hurt, and will do none,

That do not do the thing, they most do show,

Who, moving others, are themselves as stone,

Unmoved, cold, and to temptation slow,

They rightly do inherit heaven's graces

And husband nature's riches from expense;

Tibey are the lords and owners of their faces,

Others but stewards of their excellence.

The summer's flower is to the summer sweet,

Though to itself it only live and die,

But if that flower with base infection meet,

The basest weed outbraves his dignity:

For sweetest things turn sourest by their deeds;

Lilies that fester, smell far worse than weeds.

九四

谁有力量损害人而不这样干，
谁不做人以为他们爱做的事，
谁使人动情，自己却石头一般，
冰冷、无动于衷，对诱惑能抗拒——

谁就恰当地承受上天的恩宠，
善于贮藏和保管造化的财富；
他们才是自己美貌的主人翁，
而别人只是自己姿色的家奴。

夏天的花把夏天熏得多芳馥，
虽然对自己它只自开又自落，
但是那花若染上卑劣的病毒，
最贱的野草也比它高贵得多。

极香的东西一腐烂就成极臭，
烂百合花比野草更臭得难受。

Sonnet 95

How sweet and lovely dost thou make the shame

Which, like a canker in the fragrant rose,

Doth spot the beauty of thy budding name!

O! in what sweets dost thou thy sins enclose.

That tongue that tells the story of thy days,

Making lascivious comments on thy sport,

Cannot dispraise, but in a kind of praise;

Naming thy name blesses an ill report.

O! what a mansion have those vices got

Which for their habitation chose out thee,

Where beauty's veil doth cover every blot

And all things turns to fair that eyes can see!

Take heed, dear heart, of this large privilege;

The hardest knife ill-used doth lose his edge.

九五

耻辱被你弄成多温柔多可爱！
恰像馥郁的玫瑰花心的毛虫，
它把你含苞欲放的美名污败！
哦，多少温馨把你的罪过遮蒙！

那讲述你的生平故事的长舌，
想对你的娱乐作淫猥的评论，
只能用一种赞美口气来贬责：
一提起你名字，诬蔑也变谄佞。

哦，那些罪过找到了多大的华厦，
当它们把你挑选来作安乐窝，
在那儿美为污点披上了轻纱，
在那儿触目的一切都变清和！

警惕呵，心肝，为你这特权警惕；
最快的刀被滥用也失去锋利！

Sonnet 96

Some say thy fault is youth, some wantonness;
Some say thy grace is youth and gentle sport;
Both grace and faults are loved of more and less:
Thou mak'st faults graces, that to thee resort.

As on the finger of a throned queen
The basest jewel will be well esteemed,
So are those errors that in thee are seen
To truths translated, and for true things deemed.

How many lambs might the stern wolf betray,
If like a lamb he could his looks translate!
How many gazers mightst thou lead away,
If thou wouldst use the strength of all thy state!

But do not so; I love thee in such sort,
As, thou being mine, mine is thy good report.

九六

有人说你的缺点在年少放荡；
有人说你的魅力在年少风流；
魅力和缺点都多少受人赞赏，
缺点变成添在魅力上的锦绣。

宝座上的女王手上戴的戒指，
就是最贱的宝石也受人尊重，
同样，那在你身上出现的瑕疵
也变成真理，当作真理被推崇。

多少绵羊会受到野狼的引诱，
假如野狼戴上了绵羊的面目！
多少爱慕你的人会被你拐走，
假如你肯把你全部力量使出！

可别这样做。我既然这样爱你，
你是我的，我的光荣也属于你。

Sonnet 97

How like a winter hath my absence been

From thee, the pleasure of the fleeting year!

What freezings have I felt, what dark days seen!

What old December's bareness everywhere!

And yet this time removed was summer's time,

The teeming autumn, big with rich increase,

Bearing the wanton burden of the prime,

Like widowed wombs after their lords' decease.

Yet this abundant issue seemed to me

But hope of orphans and unfathered fruit;

For summer and his pleasures wait on thee,

And, thou away, the very birds are mute.

Or, if they sing, 'tis with so dull a cheer,

That leaves look pale, dreading the winter's near.

九七

离开了你，日子多么像严冬，
你，飞逝的流年中唯一的欢乐！
天色多阴暗！我又受尽了寒冻！
触目是龙钟腊月的一片萧索！

可是别离的时期恰好是夏日，
和膨胀着累累的丰收的秋天，
满载着青春的淫荡结下的果实，
好像怀胎的新寡妇，大腹便便。

但是这累累的丰收，在我看来，
只能成无父孤儿和乖异的果；
因夏天和它的欢娱把你款待，
你不在，连小鸟也停止了唱歌。

或者，即使它们唱，声调那么沉，
树叶全变灰了，生怕冬天降临。

Sonnet 98

From you have I been absent in the spring,

When proud-pied April, dressed in all his trim,

Hath put a spirit of youth in everything,

That heavy Saturn laughed and leaped with him.

Yet nor the lays of birds nor the sweet smell

Of different flowers in odour and in hue,

Could make me any summer's story tell,

Or from their proud lap pluck them where they grew;

Nor did I wonder at the lily's white,

Nor praise the deep vermilion in the rose;

They were but sweet, but figures of delight;

Drawn after you, you pattern of all those.

Yet seemed it winter still, and, you away,

As with your shadow I with these did play.

九八

我离开你的时候正好是春天，
当绚烂的四月，披上新的锦袄，
把活泼的春心给万物灌注遍，
连沉重的土星①也跟着笑和跳。

可是无论小鸟的歌唱，或万紫
千红、芬芳四溢的一簇簇鲜花，
都不能使我诉说夏天的故事，
或从烂熳的山洼把它们采掐。

我也不羡慕那百合花的洁白，
也不赞美玫瑰花的一片红晕；
它们不过是香，是悦目的雕刻，
你才是它们所要摹拟的真身。

因此，于我还是严冬，而你不在，
像逗着你影子，我逗它们开怀。

---

① 土星在西欧星相学里是沉闷和忧郁的象征。

Sonnet 99

The forward violet thus did I chide,

Sweet thief, whence didst thou steal thy sweet that smells,

If not from my love's breath? The purple pride

Which on thy soft check for complexion dwells,

In my love's veins thou hast too grossly dyed.

The lily I condemned for thy hand,

And buds of marjoram had stol'n thy hair,

The roses fearfully on thorns did stand,

One blushing shame, another white despair;

A third, nor red nor white, had stol'n of both

And to his robbery had annexed thy breath;

But, for his theft, in pride of all his growth

A vengeful canker eat him up to death.

More flowers I noted, yet I none could see

But sweet or colour it had stol'n from thee.

九九

我对孟浪的紫罗兰这样谴责：
"温柔贼，你哪里偷来这缕温馨，
若不是从我爱的呼吸？这紫色
在你的柔颊上抹了一层红晕，
还不是从我爱的血管里染得？"

我申斥百合花盗用了你的手，
茉沃兰的蓓蕾偷取你的柔发；
站在刺上的玫瑰花吓得直抖，
一朵羞得通红，一朵绝望到发白。

另一朵，不红不白，从双方偷来，
还在赃物上添上了你的呼吸；
但既犯了盗窃，当它正昂头盛开，
一条怒冲冲的毛虫把它咬死。

我还看见许多花，但没有一朵
不从你那里偷取芬芳和婀娜。

Sonnet 100

Where art thou, Muse, that thou forget'st so long

To speak of that which gives thee all thy might?

Spend'st thou thy fury on some worthless song,

Darkening thy power to lend base subjects light?

Return, forgetful Muse, and straight redeem

In gentle numbers time so idly spent;

Sing to the ear that doth thy lays esteem

And gives thy pen both skill and argument.

Rise, resty Muse, my love's sweet face survey,

If time have any wrinkle graven there;

If any, be a satire to decay,

And make time's spoils despised everywhere.

Give my love fame faster than Time wastes life;

So thou prevent'st his scythe and crooked knife.

一〇〇

你在哪里，诗神，竟长期忘记掉
把你的一切力量的源头歌唱？
为什么浪费狂热于一些滥调，
消耗你的光去把俗物照亮？

回来吧，健忘的诗神，立刻轻弹
宛转的旋律，赎回虚度的光阴；
唱给那衷心爱慕你并把灵感
和技巧赐给你的笔的耳朵听。

起来，懒诗神，检查我爱的秀容，
看时光可曾在那里刻下皱纹；
假如有，就要尽量把衰老嘲讽，
使时光的剽窃到处遭人齿冷。

快使爱成名，趁时光未下手前，
你就挡得住它的风刀和霜剑。

Sonnet 101

O, truant Muse, what shall be thy amends
For thy neglect of truth in beauty dyed?
Both truth and beauty on my love depends;
So dost thou too, and therein dignified.

Make answer Muse, wilt thou not haply say,
'Truth needs no colour, with his colour fixed;
Beauty no pencil, beauty's truth to lay;
But best is best, if never intermixed'?

Because he needs no praise, wilt thou be dumb?
Excuse not silence so, for't lies in thee
To make him much outlive a gilded tomb
And to be praised of ages yet to be.

Then do thy office, Muse; I teach thee how
To make him seem, long hence, as he shows now.

一〇一

偷懒的诗神呵，你将怎样补救
你对那被美渲染的真的怠慢？
真和美都与我的爱相依相守；
你也一样，要倚靠它才得通显。

说吧，诗神。你或许会这样回答：
"真的固定色彩不必用色彩绘；
美也不用翰墨把美的真容画；
用不着搀杂，完美永远是完美。"

难道他不需要赞美，你就不作声？
别替缄默辩护，因为你有力量
使他比镀金的坟墓更享遐龄，
并在未来的年代永受人赞扬。

当仁不让吧，诗神，我要教你怎样
使他今后和现在一样受景仰。

Sonnet 102

My love is strengthened, though more weak in seeming;

I love not less, though less the show appear;

That love is merchandized, whose rich esteeming,

The owner's tongue doth publish every where.

Our love was new, and then but in the spring,

When I was wont to greet it with my lays;

As Philomel in summer's front doth sing,

And stops her pipe in growth of riper days.

Not that the summer is less pleasant now

Than when her mournful hymns did hush the night,

But that wild music burthens every bough,

And sweets grown common lose their dear delight.

Therefore like her, I sometime hold my tongue,

Because I would not dull you with my song.

一〇二

我的爱加强了，虽然看来更弱；
我的爱一样热，虽然表面稍冷。
谁把他心中的崇拜到处传播，
就等于把他的爱情看作商品。

我们那时才新恋，又正当春天，
我惯用我的歌去欢迎它来归，
像夜莺在夏天门前彻夜清啭，
到了盛夏的日子便停止歌吹。

并非现在夏天没有那么惬意，
比起万籁静听它哀唱的时候，
只为狂欢的音乐载满每一枝，
太普通，意味便没有那么深悠。

所以，像它，我有时也默默无言，
免得我的歌，太繁了，使你烦厌。

Sonnet 103

Alack! what poverty my muse brings forth,

That having such a scope to show her pride,

The argument all bare is of more worth

Than when it hath my added praise beside!

O! blame me not if I no more can write!

Look in your glass, and there appears a face

That over-goes my blunt invention quite,

Dulling my lines, and doing me disgrace.

Were it not sinful then, striving to mend,

To mar the subject that before was well?

For to no other pass my verses tend

Than of your graces and your gifts to tell;

And more, much more, than in my verse can sit,

Your own glass shows you when you look in it.

一〇三

我的诗神的产品多贫乏可怜!
分明有无限天地可炫耀才华,
可是她的题材,尽管一无妆点,
比加上我的赞美价值还要大!

别非难我,如果我写不出什么!
照照镜子吧,看你镜中的面孔
多么超越我的怪笨拙的创作,
使我的诗失色,叫我无地自容。

那可不是罪过吗,努力要增饰,
反而把原来无瑕的题材涂毁?
因为我的诗并没有其他目的,
除了要模仿你的才情和妩媚。

是的,你的镜子,当你向它端详,
所反映的远远多于我的诗章。

Sonnet 104

To me, fair friend, you never can be old,

For as you were when first your eye I eyed,

Such seems your beauty still. three winters cold,

Have from the forests shook three summers' pride,

Three beauteous springs to yellow autumn turned,

In process of the seasons have I seen,

Three April perfumes in three hot Junes burned,

Since first I saw you fresh, which yet are green.

Ah! yet doth beauty like a dial-hand,

Steal from his figure, and no pace perceived;

So your sweet hue, which methinks still doth stand,

Hath motion, and mine eye may be deceived.

For fear of which, hear this thou age unbred,

Ere you were born was beauty's summer dead.

一〇四

对于我，俊友，你永远不会衰老，
因为自从我的眼碰见你的眼，
你还是一样美。三个严冬摇掉
三个苍翠的夏天的树叶和光艳，

三个阳春三度化作秋天的枯黄。
时序使我三度看见四月的芳菲
三度被六月的炎炎烈火烧光。
但你，还是和初见时一样明媚；

唉，可是美，像时针，它蹑着脚步
移过钟面，你看不见它的踪影；
同样，你的姣颜，我以为是常驻，
其实在移动，迷惑的是我的眼睛。

颤栗吧，未来的时代，听我呼吁：
你还没有生，美的夏天已死去。

Sonnet 105

Let not my love be called idolatry,

Nor my beloved as an idol show,

Since all alike my songs and praises be

To one, of one, still such, and ever so.

Kind is my love today, tomorrow kind,

Still constant in a wondrous excellence;

Therefore my verse to constancy confined,

One thing expressing, leaves out difference.

Fair, kind, and true, is all my argument,

Fair, kind, and true, varying to other words;

And in this change is my invention spent,

Three themes in one, which wondrous scope affords.

Fair, kind, and true, have often lived alone,

Which three till now, never kept seat in one.

一〇五

不要把我的爱叫作偶像崇拜，
也不要把我的爱人当偶像看，
既然所有我的歌和我的赞美
都献给一个、为一个，永无变换。

我的爱今天仁慈，明天也仁慈，
有着惊人的美德，永远不变心，
所以我的诗也一样坚贞不渝，
全省掉差异，只叙述一件事情。

"美、善和真"，就是我全部的题材，
"美、善和真"，用不同的词句表现；
我的创造就在这变化上演才，
三题一体，它的境界可真无限。

过去"美、善和真"常常分道扬镳，
到今天才在一个人身上协调。

Sonnet 106

When in the chronicle of wasted time
I see descriptions of the fairest wights,
And beauty making beautiful old rhyme,
In praise of ladies dead, and lovely knights;

Then in the blazon of sweet beauty's best,
Of hand, of foot, of lip, of eye, of brow,
I see their antique pen would have expressed
Even such a beauty as you master now.

So all their praises are but prophecies
Of this our time, all you prefiguring;
And for they looked but with divining eyes,
They had not skill enough your worth to sing:

For we, which now behold these present days,
Have eyes to wonder, but lack tongues to praise.

一〇六

当我从那湮远的古代的纪年
发现那绝代风流人物的写真,
艳色使得古老的歌咏也香艳,
颂赞着多情骑士和绝命佳人。

于是,从那些国色天姿的描画,
无论手脚、嘴唇,或眼睛或眉额,
我发觉那些古拙的笔所表达
恰好是你现在所占领的姿色。

所以他们的赞美无非是预言
我们这时代,一切都预告着你;
不过他们观察只用想象的眼,
还不够才华把你歌颂得尽致。

而我们,幸而得亲眼看见今天,
只有眼惊羡,却没有舌头咏叹。

Sonnet 107

Not mine own fears, nor the prophetic soul

Of the wide world dreaming on things to come,

Can yet the lease of my true love control,

Supposed as forfeit to a confined doom.

The mortal moon hath her eclipse endured,

And the sad augurs mock their own presage;

Incertainties now crown themselves assured,

And peace proclaims olives of endless age.

Now with the drops of this most balmy time,

My love looks fresh, and Death to me subscribes,

Since, spite of him, I'll live in this poor rhyme,

While he insults o'er dull and speechless tribes:

And thou in this shalt find thy monument,

When tyrants' crests and tombs of brass are spent.

一〇七

无论我自己的忧虑，或那梦想着
未来的这茫茫世界的先知灵魂，
都不能限制我的真爱的租约，
纵使它已注定作命运的抵偿品。

人间的月亮已度过被蚀的灾难，
不祥的占卜把自己的预言嘲讽，
动荡和疑虑既已获得了保险，
和平在宣告橄榄枝永久葱茏。

于是在这时代甘露的遍洒下，
我的爱面貌一新，而死神降伏，
既然我将活在这拙作里，任凭他
把那些愚钝的无言的种族凌辱。

你将在这里找着你的纪念碑，
魔王的金盔和铜墓却被销毁。

Sonnet 108

What's in the brain, that ink may character,

Which hath not figured to thee my true spirit?

What's new to speak, what now to register,

That may express my love, or thy dear merit?

Nothing, sweet boy; but yet like prayers divine,

I must each day say o'er the very same;

Counting no old thing old, thou mine, I thine,

Even as when first I hallowed thy fair name.

So that eternal love in love's fresh case,

Weighs not the dust and injury of age,

Nor gives to necessary wrinkles place,

But makes antiquity for aye his page:

Finding the first conceit of love there bred,

Where time and outward form would show it dead.

一〇八

脑袋里有什么，笔墨形容得出，
我这颗真心不已经对你描画？
还有什么新东西可说可记录，
以表白我的爱或者你的真价？

没有，乖乖。可是，虔诚的祷词
我没有一天不把它复说一遍；
老话并不老。你属我，我也属你，
就像我祝福你名字的头一天。

所以永恒的爱在长青爱匣里
不会蒙受年岁的损害和尘土，
不会让皱纹占据应有的位置，
反而把老时光当作永久的家奴；

发觉最初的爱苗依旧得保养，
尽管时光和外貌都盼它枯黄。

Sonnet 109

O never say that I was false of heart,

Though absence seemed my flame to qualify,

As easy might I from myself depart

As from my soul which in thy breast doth lie.

That is my home of love, if I have ranged,

Like him that travels, I return again;

Just to the time, not with the time exchanged,

So that myself bring water for my stain.

Never believe though in my nature reigned,

All frailties that besiege all kinds of blood,

That it could so preposterously be stained,

To leave for nothing all thy sum of good;

For nothing this wide universe I call,

Save thou, my rose, in it thou art my all.

一〇九

哦，千万别埋怨我改变过心肠，
别离虽似乎减低了我的热情。
正如我抛不开自己远走他方，
我也一刻离不开你，我的灵魂。

你是我的爱的家：我虽曾流浪，
现在已经像远行的游子归来；
并准时到家，没有跟时光改样，
而且把洗涤我污点的水带来。

哦，请千万别相信（尽管我难免
和别人一样经不起各种试诱）
我的天性会那么荒唐和鄙贱，
竟抛弃你这至宝去追求乌有。

这无垠的宇宙对我都是虚幻，
你才是，我的玫瑰，我全部财产。

Sonnet 110

Alas! 'tis true, I have gone here and there,
And made myself a motley to the view,
Gored mine own thoughts, sold cheap what is most dear,
Made old offences of affections new;

Most true it is, that I have looked on truth
Askance and strangely; but, by all above,
These blenches gave my heart another youth,
And worse essays proved thee my best of love.

Now all is done, have what shall have no end,
Mine appetite I never more will grind
On newer proof, to try an older friend,
A god in love, to whom I am confined.

Then give me welcome, next my heaven the best,
Even to thy pure and most most loving breast.

一一〇

唉，我的确曾经常东奔西跑，
扮作斑衣的小丑供众人赏玩，
违背我的意志，把至宝贱卖掉，
为了新交不惜把旧知交冒犯；

更千真万确我曾经斜着冷眼
去看真情；但天呀，这种种离乖
给我的心带来了另一个春天，
最坏的考验证实了你的真爱。

现在一切都过去了，请你接受
无尽的友谊：我不再把欲望磨利，
用新的试探去考验我的老友——
那拘禁我的、钟情于我的神祇。

那么，欢迎我吧，我的人间的天，
迎接我到你最亲的纯洁的胸间。

Sonnet 111

O! for my sake do you with Fortune chide,

The guilty goddess of my harmful deeds,

That did not better for my life provide

Than public means which public manners breeds.

Thence comes it that my name receives a brand,

And almost thence my nature is subdued

To what it works in, like the dyer's hand.

Pity me, then, and wish I were renewed;

Whilst, like a willing patient, I will drink

Potions of eisel 'gainst my strong infection;

No bitterness that I will bitter think,

Nor double penance, to correct correction.

Pity me then, dear friend, and I assure ye,

Even that your pity is enough to cure me.

———

哦，请为我把命运的女神诟让，
她是嗾使我造成业障的主犯，
因为她对我的生活别无赡养，
除了养成我粗鄙的众人米饭。

因而我的名字就把烙印① 接受，
也几乎为了这缘故我的天性
被职业所玷污，如同染工的手：
可怜我吧，并祝福我获得更新；

像个温顺的病人，我甘心饮服
涩嘴的醋来消除我的重感染②；
不管它多苦，我将一点不觉苦，
也不辞两重忏悔以赎我的罪愆。

请怜悯我吧，挚友，我向你担保
你的怜悯已经够把我医治好。

———

① 烙印：耻辱。
② 当时的人相信醋能防疫。

Sonnet 112

Your love and pity doth th' impression fill,

Which vulgar scandal stamped upon my brow;

For what care I who calls me well or ill,

So you o'er-green my bad, my good allow?

You are my all-the-world, and I must strive

To know my shames and praises from your tongue;

None else to me, nor I to none alive,

That my steeled sense or changes right or wrong.

In so profound abysm I throw all care

Of others' voices, that my adder's sense

To critic and to flatterer stopped are.

Mark how with my neglect I do dispense:

You are so strongly in my purpose bred,

That all the world besides methinks are dead.

一一二

你的爱怜抹掉那世俗的讥谗
打在我的额上的耻辱的烙印；
别人的毁誉对我有什么相干，
你既表扬我的善又把恶遮隐！

你是我整个宇宙，我必须努力
从你的口里听取我的荣和辱；
我把别人，别人把我，都当作死，
谁能使我的铁心肠变善或变恶？

别人的意见我全扔入了深渊，
那么干净，我简直像聋蛇一般，
凭他奉承或诽谤都充耳不闻。
请倾听我怎样原谅我的冷淡：

你那么根深蒂固长在我心里，
全世界，除了你，我都认为死去。

Sonnet 113

Since I left you, mine eye is in my mind;

And that which governs me to go about

Doth part his function and is partly blind,

Seems seeing, but effectually is out;

For it no form delivers to the heart

Of bird, of flower, or shape which it doth latch,

Of his quick objects hath the mind no part,

Nor his own vision holds what it doth catch;

For if it see the rud'st or gentlest sight,

The most sweet favour or deformed'st creature,

The mountain or the sea, the day or night,

The crow, or dove, it shapes them to your feature.

Incapable of more, replete with you,

My most true mind thus maketh mine untrue.

一一三

自从离开你，眼睛便移居心里，
于是那双指挥我行动的眼睛，
既把职守分开，就成了半瞎子，
自以为还看见，其实已经失明；

因为它们所接触的任何形状，
花鸟或姿态，都不能再传给心，
自己也留不住把捉到的景象；
一切过眼的事物心儿都无份。

因为一见粗俗或幽雅的景色，
最畸形的怪物或绝艳的面孔，
山或海，日或夜，乌鸦或者白鸽，
眼睛立刻塑成你美妙的姿容。

心中满是你，什么再也装不下，
就这样我的真心教眼睛说假话。

Sonnet 114

Or whether doth my mind, being crowned with you,

Drink up the monarch's plague, this flattery?

Or whether shall I say, mine eye saith true,

And that your love taught it this alchemy,

To make of monsters and things indigest

Such cherubins as your sweet self resemble,

Creating every bad a perfect best,

As fast as objects to his beams assemble?

O! 'tis the first, 'tis flattery in my seeing,

And my great mind most kingly drinks it up,

Mine eye well knows what with his gust is 'greeing,

And to his palate doth prepare the cup.

If it be poisoned, 'tis the lesser sin

That mine eye loves it and doth first begin.

一一四

是否我的心，既把你当王冠戴，
喝过帝王们的鸩毒——自我阿谀？
还是我该说，我眼睛说的全对，
因为你的爱教会它这炼金术，

使它能够把一切蛇神和牛鬼
转化为和你一样柔媚的天婴，
把每个丑恶改造成尽善尽美，
只要事物在它的柔辉下现形？

哦，是前者。是眼睛的自我陶醉，
我伟大的心灵把它一口喝尽：
眼睛晓得投合我心灵的口味，
为它准备好这杯可口的毒饮。

尽管杯中有毒，罪过总比较轻，
因为先爱上它的是我的眼睛。

Sonnet 115

Those lines that I before have writ do lie,

Even those that said I could not love you dearer,

Yet then my judgment knew no reason why

My most full flame should afterwards burn clearer.

But reckoning time, whose millioned accidents

Creep in 'twixt vows, and change decrees of kings,

Tan sacred beauty, blunt the sharp'st intents,

Divert strong minds to the course of altering things;

Alas! why, fearing of time's tyranny,

Might I not then say, 'Now I love you best,'

When I was certain o'er incertainty,

Crowning the present, doubting of the rest?

Love is a babe, then might I not say so,

To give full growth to that which still doth grow?

一一五

我从前写的那些诗全都撒谎，
连那些说"我爱你到极点"在内，
可是那时候我的确无法想象
白热的火还发得出更大光辉。

只害怕时光的无数意外事故
钻进密约间，勾销帝王的意旨，
晒黑美色，并挫钝锋锐的企图，
使倔强的心屈从事物的隆替：

唉，为什么，既怵于时光的专横，
我不可说，"现在我爱你到极点"，
当我摆脱掉疑虑，充满着信心，
觉得来日不可期，只掌握目前？

爱是婴儿。难道我不可这样讲，
去促使在生长中的羽毛丰满？

Sonnet 116

Let me not to the marriage of true minds

Admit impediments. Love is not love

Which alters when it alteration finds,

Or bends with the remover to remove.

O no! it is an ever-fixed mark

That looks on tempests and is never shaken;

It is the star to every wandering bark,

Whose worth's unknown, although his height be taken.

Love's not Time's fool, though rosy lips and cheeks

Within his bending sickle's compass come,

Love alters not with his brief hours and weeks,

But bears it out even to the edge of doom.

If this be error and upon me proved,

I never writ, nor no man ever loved.

一一六

我绝不承认两颗真心的结合
会有任何障碍；爱算不得真爱，
若是一看见人家改变便转舵，
或者一看见人家转弯便离开。

哦，绝不！爱是亘古长明的塔灯，
它定睛望着风暴却兀不为动；
爱又是指引迷舟的一颗恒星，
你可量它多高，它所值却无穷。

爱不受时光的播弄，尽管红颜
和皓齿难免遭受时光的毒手；
爱并不因瞬息的改变而改变，
它巍然矗立直到末日的尽头。

我这话若说错，并被证明不确，
就算我没写诗，也没人真爱过。

Sonnet 117

Accuse me thus, that I have scanted all,

Wherein I should your great deserts repay,

Forgot upon your dearest love to call,

Whereto all bonds do tie me day by day;

That I have frequent been with unknown minds,

And given to time your own dear-purchased right;

That I have hoisted sail to all the winds

Which should transport me farthest from your sight.

Book both my wilfulness and errors down,

And on just proof surmise, accumulate;

Bring me within the level of your frown,

But shoot not at me in your wakened hate;

Since my appeal says I did strive to prove

The constancy and virtue of your love.

一一七

请这样控告我：说我默不作声，
尽管对你的深恩我应当酬谢；
说我忘记向你缱绻的爱慰问，
尽管我对你依恋一天天密切；

说我时常和陌生的心灵来往，
为偶尔机缘断送你宝贵情谊；
说我不管什么风都把帆高扬，
任它们把我吹到天涯海角去。

请把我的任性和错误都记下，
在真凭实据上还要积累嫌疑，
把我带到你的颦眉蹙额底下，
千万别唤醒怨毒来把我射死；

因为我的诉状说我急于证明
你对我的爱多么忠贞和坚定。

Sonnet 118

Like as, to make our appetite more keen,

With eager compounds we our palate urge,

As, to prevent our maladies unseen,

We sicken to shun sickness when we purge;

Even so, being full of your ne'er-cloying sweetness,

To bitter sauces did I frame my feeding;

And, sick of welfare, found a kind of meetness

To be diseased, ere that there was true needing.

Thus policy in love, to anticipate

The ills that were not, grew to faults assured,

And brought to medicine a healthful state

Which rank of goodness, would by ill be cured;

But thence I learn and find the lesson true,

Drugs poison him that so feil sick of you.

一一八

好比我们为了促使食欲增进，
用种种辛辣调味品刺激胃口；
又好比服清泻剂以预防大病，
用较轻的病截断重症的根由；

同样，饱尝了你的不腻人的甜蜜，
我选上苦酱来当作我的食料；
厌倦了健康，觉得病也有意思，
尽管我还没有到生病的必要。

这样，为采用先发制病的手段，
爱的策略变成了真实的过失。
我对健康的身体乱投下药丹，
用痛苦来把过度的幸福疗治。

但我由此取得这真正的教训：
药也会变毒，谁若因爱你而生病。

Sonnet 119

What potions have I drunk of Siren tears,

Distilled from limbecks foul as hell within,

Applying fears to hopes, and hopes to fears,

Still losing when I saw myself to win!

What wretched errors hath my heart committed,

Whilst it hath thought itself so blessed never!

How have mine eyes out of their spheres been fitted,

In the distraction of this madding fever!

O, benefit of ill, now I find true

That better is by evil still made better.

And ruined love, when it is built anew

Grows fairer than at first, more strong, far greater,

So I return rebuked to my content,

And gain by ills thrice more than I have spent.

一一九

我曾喝下了多少鲛人的泪珠，
从我心中地狱般的锅里蒸出来，
把恐惧当希望，又把希望当恐惧，
眼看着要胜利，结果还是失败！

我的心犯了多少可怜的错误，
正好当它自以为再幸福不过；
我的眼睛怎样地从眼眶跃出，
当我被疯狂昏乱的热病折磨！

哦，坏事变好事！我现在才知道
善的确常常因恶而变得更善！
被摧毁的爱，一旦重新修建好，
就比原来更宏伟、更美、更强顽。

因此，我受了谴责，反心满意足；
因祸，我获得过去的三倍幸福。

Sonnet 120

That you were once unkind befriends me now,

And for that sorrow, which I then did feel,

Needs must I under my transgression bow,

Unless my nerves were brass or hammered steel.

For if you were by my unkindness shaken,

As I by yours, you've passed a hell of time;

And I, a tyrant, have no leisure taken

To weigh how once I suffered in your crime.

O, that our night of woe might have remembered

My deepest sense, how hard true sorrow hits,

And soon to you, as you to me, then tendered

The humble salve which wounded bosoms fits!

But that your trespass now becomes a fee;

Mine ransoms yours, and yours must ransom me.

一二〇

你对我狠过心反而于我有利：
想起你当时使我受到的痛创，
我只好在我的过失下把头低，
既然我的神经不是铜或精钢。

因为，你若受过我狠心的摇撼，
像我所受的，该熬过多苦的日子！
可是我这暴君从没有抽过闲
来衡量你的罪行对我的打击！

哦，但愿我们那悲怆之夜能使我
牢牢记住真悲哀打击得多惨，
我就会立刻递给你，像你递给我，
那抚慰碎了的心的微贱药丹。

但你的罪行现在变成了保证，
我赎你的罪，你也赎我的败行。

Sonnet 121

'Tis better to be vile than vile esteemed,

When not to be, receives reproach of being;

And the just pleasure lost, which is so deemed

Not by our feeling, but by others' seeing.

For why should others' false adulterate eyes

Give salutation to my sportive blood?

Or on my frailties why are frailer spies,

Which in their wills count bad what I think good?

No, I am that I am, and they that level

At my abuses reckon up their own,

I may be straight though they themselves be bevel;

By their rank thoughts, my deeds must not be shown;

Unless this general evil they maintain,

All men are bad and in their badness reign.

一二一

宁可卑劣，也不愿负卑劣的虚名，
当我们的清白蒙上不白之冤，
当正当的娱乐被人妄加恶声，
不体察我们的感情，只凭偏见。

为什么别人虚伪淫猥的眼睛
有权赞扬或诋毁我活跃的血？
专侦伺我的弱点而比我坏的人
为什么把我认为善的恣意污蔑？

我就是我，他们对于我的诋毁
只能够宣扬他们自己的卑鄙。
我本方正，他们的视线自不轨，
这种坏心眼怎么配把我非议？

除非他们固执这糊涂的邪说：
恶是人性，统治着世间的是恶。

Sonnet 122

Thy gift, thy tables, are within my brain

Full charactered with lasting memory,

Which shall above that idle rank remain

Beyond all date even to eternity.

Or, at the least, so long as brain and heart

Have faculty by nature to subsist;

Till each to razed oblivion yield his part

Of thee, thy record never can be missed.

That poor retention could not so much hold,

Nor need I tallies thy dear love to score;

Therefore to give them from me was I bold,

To trust those tables that receive thee more.

To keep an adjunct to remember thee

Were to import forgetfulness in me.

一二二

你赠我的手册已经一笔一划
永不磨灭地刻在我的心版上，
它将超越无聊的名位的高下，
跨过一切时代，以至无穷无疆。

或者，至少直到大自然的规律
容许心和脑继续存在的一天；
直到它们把你每部分都让给
遗忘，你的记忆将永远不逸散。

可怜的手册就无法那样持久，
我也不用筹码把你的爱登记；
所以你的手册我大胆地放走，
把你交给更能珍藏你的册子。

要靠备忘录才不会把你遗忘，
岂不等于表明我对你也善忘？

Sonnet 123

No! Time, thou shalt not boast that I do change,

Thy pyramids built up with newer might

To me are nothing novel, nothing strange;

They are but dressings of a former sight.

Our dates are brief, and therefore we admire

What thou dost foist upon us that is old,

And rather make them born to our desire

Than think that we before have heard them told.

Thy registers and thee I both defy,

Not wondering at the present nor the past,

For thy records and what we see doth lie,

Made more or less by thy continual haste.

This I do vow and this shall ever be;

I will be true, despite thy scythe and thee.

一二三

不，时光，你断不能夸说我在变。
你新建的金字塔，不管多雄壮，
对我一点不稀奇，一点不新鲜；
它们只是旧景象披上了新装。

我们的生命太短促，所以羡慕
你拿来蒙骗我们的那些旧货；
幻想它们是我们心愿的产物，
不肯信从前曾经有人谈起过。

对你和你的纪录我同样不买账，
过去和现在都不能使我惊奇，
因为你的记载和我所见都扯谎，
都多少是你疾驰中造下的孽迹。

我敢这样发誓：我将万古不渝，
不管你和你的镰刀多么锋利。

Sonnet 124

If my dear love were but the child of state,

It might for Fortune's bastard be unfathered,

As subject to time's love or to time's hate,

Weeds among weeds, or flowers with flowers gathered.

No, it was builded far from accident;

It suffers not in smiling pomp, nor falls

Under the blow of thralled discontent,

Whereto th' inviting time our fashion calls.

It fears not policy, that heretic,

Which works on leases of short-numbered hours,

But all alone stands hugely politic,

That it nor grows with heat, nor drowns with showers.

To this I witness call the fools of time,

Which die for goodness, who have lived for crime.

一二四

假如我的爱只是权势的嫡种，
它就会是命运的无父的私生子，
受时光的宠辱所磨折和播弄，
同野草闲花一起任人们采刈。

不呀，它并不是建立在偶然上；
它既不为荣华的笑颜所转移，
也经受得起我们这时代风尚
司空见惯的抑郁、愤懑的打击。

它不害怕那只在短期间有效、
到处散播异端和邪说的权谋，
不因骄阳而生长，雨也冲不掉，
它巍然独立在那里，深思熟筹。

被时光愚弄的人们，起来作证！
你们毕生作恶，却一死得干净。

Sonnet 125

Were't aught to me I bore the canopy,

With my extern the outward honouring,

Or laid great bases for eternity,

Which proves more short than waste or ruining?

Have I not seen dwellers on form and favour

Lose all and more by paying too much rent

For compound sweet; forgoing simple savour,

Pitiful thrivers, in their gazing spent?

No; let me be obsequious in thy heart,

And take thou my oblation, poor but free,

Which is not mixed with seconds, knows no art,

But mutual render, only me for thee.

Hence, thou suborned informer! a true soul

When most impeached, stands least in thy control.

一二五

这对我何益，纵使我高擎华盖，
用我的外表来为你妆点门面，
或奠下伟大基础，要留芳万代，
其实比荒凉和毁灭为期更短？

难道我没见过拘守仪表的人，
付出高昂的代价，却丧失一切，
厌弃淡泊而拼命去追求荤辛，
可怜的赢利者，在顾盼中凋谢？

不，请让我在你心里长保忠贞，
收下这份菲薄但由衷的献礼，
它不搀杂次品，也不包藏机心，
而只是你我间互相致送诚意。

被收买的告密者，滚开！你越诬告
真挚的心，越不能损害它分毫。

Sonnet 126

O thou, my lovely boy, who in thy power

Dost hold Time's fickle glass, his fickle, hour;

Who hast by waning grown, and therein show'st

Thy lovers withering, as thy sweet self grow'st.

If Nature, sovereign mistress over wrack,

As thou goest onwards, still will pluck thee back,

She keeps thee to this purpose, that her skill

May time disgrace and wretched minutes kill.

Yet fear her, O thou minion of her pleasure!

She may detain, but not still keep, her treasure:

Her audit, though delayed, answered must be,

And her quietus is to render thee.

一二六

你，小乖乖，时光的无常的沙漏
和时辰（他的小镰刀）都听你左右；
你在亏缺中生长，并昭示大众
你的爱人如何凋零而你向荣；

如果造化（掌握盈亏的大主宰），
在你迈步前进时把你挽回来，
她的目的只是：卖弄她的手法
去丢时光的脸，并把分秒扼杀。

可是你得怕她，你，她的小乖乖！
她只能暂留，并非常保，她的宝贝！
她的账目，虽延了期，必须清算：
要清偿债务，她就得把你交还。

Sonnet 127

In the old age black was not counted fair,

Or if it were, it bore not beauty's name;

But now is black beauty's successive heir,

And beauty slandered with a bastard shame,

For since each hand hath put on nature's power,

Fairing the foul with art's false borrowed face,

Sweet beauty hath no name no holy bower,

But is profaned, if not lives in disgrace.

Therefore my mistress' eyes are raven black,

Her eyes so suited, and they mourners seem

At such who, not born fair, no beauty lack,

Slandering creation with a false esteem:

Yet so they mourn, becoming of their woe,

That every tongue says beauty should look so.

一二七

在远古的时代黑并不算秀俊，
即使算，也没有把美的名挂上；
但如今黑既成为美的继承人，
于是美便招来了侮辱和诽谤。

因为自从每只手都修饰自然，
用艺术的假面貌去美化丑恶，
温馨的美便失掉声价和圣殿，
纵不忍辱偷生，也遭了亵渎。

所以我情妇的头发黑如乌鸦，
眼睛也恰好相衬，就像在哀泣
那些生来不美却迷人的冤家，
用假名声去中伤造化的真誉。

这哀泣那么配合她们的悲痛，
大家齐声说：这就是美的真容。

Sonnet 128

How oft when thou, my music, music play'st,
Upon that blessed wood whose motion sounds
With thy sweet fingers when thou gently sway'st
The wiry concord that mine ear confounds,

Do I envy those jacks that nimble leap,
To kiss the tender inward of thy hand,
Whilst my poor lips which should that harvest reap,
At the wood's boldness by thee blushing stand!

To be so tickled, they would change their state
And situation with those dancing chips,
O'er whom thy fingers walk with gentle gait,
Making dead wood more blest than living lips,

Since saucy jacks so happy are in this,
Give them thy fingers, me thy lips to kiss.

一二八

多少次，我的音乐，当你在弹奏
音乐，我眼看那些幸福的琴键
跟着你那轻盈的手指的挑逗，
发出悦耳的旋律，使我魂倒神颠——

我多么艳羡那些琴键轻快地
跳起来狂吻你那温柔的掌心，
而我可怜的嘴唇，本该有这权利，
只能红着脸对琴键的放肆出神！

经不起这引逗，我嘴唇巴不得
做那些舞蹈着的得意小木片，
因为你手指在它们身上轻掠，
使枯木比活嘴唇更值得艳羡。

冒失的琴键既由此得到快乐，
请把手指给它们，把嘴唇给我。

Sonnet 129

The expense of spirit in a waste of shame

Is lust in action, and till action, lust

Is perjured, murd'rous, bloody full of blame,

Savage, extreme, rude, cruel, not to trust;

Enjoyed no sooner but despised straight;

Past reason hunted, and no sooner had,

Past reason hated, as a swallowed bait,

On purpose laid to make the taker mad.

Mad in pursuit and in possession so;

Had, having, and in quest to have, extreme;

A bliss in proof, and proved, a very woe:

Before, a joy proposed; behind a dream.

All this the world well knows; yet none knows well

To shun the heaven that leads men to this hell.

一二九

把精力消耗在耻辱的沙漠里，
就是色欲在行动；而在行动前，
色欲赌假咒、嗜血、好杀、满身是
罪恶，凶残、粗野、不可靠、走极端；

欢乐尚未央，马上就感觉无味。
毫不讲理地追求，可是一到手，
又毫不讲理地厌恶，像是专为
引上钩者发狂而设下的钓钩。

在追求时疯狂，占有时也疯狂，
不管已有、现有、未有，全不放松；
感受时，幸福；感受完，无上灾殃。
事前，巴望着的欢乐；事后，一场梦。

这一切人共知。但谁也不知怎样
逃避这个引人下地狱的天堂。

Sonnet 130

My mistress' eyes are nothing like the sun;

Coral is far more red than her lips red;

If snow be white, why then her breasts are dun;

If hairs be wires, black wires grow on her head.

I have seen roses damasked, red and white,

But no such roses see I in her cheeks;

And in some perfumes is there more delight

Than in the breath that from my mistress reeks.

I love to hear her speak, yet well I know

That music hath a far more pleasing sound;

I grant I never saw a goddess go,

My mistress, when she walks, treads on the ground.

And yet, by heaven, I think my love as rare

As any she belied with false compare.

一三〇

我情妇的眼睛一点不像太阳；
珊瑚比她的嘴唇还要红得多。
雪若算白，她的胸就暗褐无光，
发若是铁丝，她头上铁丝婆娑。

我见过红白的玫瑰，轻纱一般；
她颊上却找不到这样的玫瑰；
有许多芳香非常逗引人喜欢，
我情妇的呼吸并没有这香味。

我爱听她谈话，可是我很清楚
音乐的悦耳远胜于她的嗓子；
我承认从没有见过女神走路，
我情妇走路时候却脚踏实地。

可是，我敢指天发誓，我的爱侣
胜似任何被捧作天仙的美女。

Sonnet 131

Thou art as tyrannous, so as thou art,

As those whose beauties proudly make them cruel;

For well thou know'st to my dear doting heart

Thou art the fairest and most precious jewel.

Yet, in good faith, some say that thee behold,

Thy face hath not the power to make love groan;

To say they err I dare not be so bold,

Although I swear it to myself alone.

And to be sure that is not false I swear,

A thousand groans, but thinking on thy face,

One on another's neck, do witness bear

Thy black is fairest in my judgment's place.

In nothing art thou black save in thy deeds,

And thence this slander, as I think, proceeds.

一三一

尽管你不算美，你的暴虐并不
亚于那些因美而骄横的女人；
因为你知道我的心那么糊涂，
把你当作世上的至美和至珍。

不过，说实话，见过你的人都说，
你的脸缺少使爱呻吟的魅力；
尽管我心中发誓反对这说法，
我可还没有公开否认的勇气。

当然我发的誓一点也不欺人；
数不完的呻吟，一想起你的脸，
马上联翩而来，可以为我作证：
对于我，你的黑胜于一切秀妍。

你一点也不黑，除了你的人品，
可能为了这缘故，诽谤才流行。

Sonnet 132

Thine eyes I love, and they, as pitying me,

Knowing thy heart torment me with disdain,

Have put on black and loving mourners be,

Looking with pretty ruth upon my pain.

And truly not the morning sun of heaven

Better becomes the grey cheeks of the east,

Nor that full star that ushers in the even

Doth half that glory to the sober west,

As those two mourning eyes become thy face:

O! let it then as well beseem thy heart

To mourn for me since mourning doth thee grace,

And suit thy pity like in every part.

Then will I swear beauty herself is black,

And all they foul that thy complexion lack.

一三二

我爱上了你的眼睛；你的眼睛
晓得你的心用轻蔑把我磨折，
对我的痛苦表示柔媚的悲悯，
就披上黑色，做旖旎的哭丧者。

而的确，无论天上灿烂的朝阳
多么配合那东方苍白的面容，
或那照耀着黄昏的明星煌煌
（它照破了西方的黯淡的天空），

都不如你的脸配上那双泪眼。
哦，但愿你那颗心也一样为我
挂孝吧，既然丧服能使你增妍，
愿它和全身一样与悲悯配合。

黑是美的本质（我那时就赌咒），
一切缺少你的颜色的都是丑。

Sonnet 133

Beshrew that heart that makes my heart to groan

For that deep wound it gives my friend and me;

Is't not enough to torture me alone,

But slave to slavery my sweet'st friend must be?

Me from myself thy cruel eye hath taken,

And my next self thou harder hast engrossed,

Of him, myself, and thee I am forsaken;

A torment thrice three-fold thus to be crossed.

Prison my heart in thy steel bosom's ward,

But then my friend's heart let my poor heart bail;

Whoe'er keeps me, let my heart be his guard;

Thou canst not then use rigour in my gaol:

And yet thou wilt, for I being pent in thee,

Perforce am thine, and all that is in me.

一三三

那使我的心呻吟的心该诅咒，
为了它给我和我的朋友的伤痕！
难道光是折磨我一个还不够？
还要把朋友贬为奴隶的身分？

你冷酷的眼睛已夺走我自己，
那另一个我你又无情地霸占；
我已经被他（我自己）和你抛弃；
这使我遭受三三九倍的苦难。

请用你的铁心把我的心包围，
让我可怜的心保释朋友的心；
不管谁监视我，我都把他保卫，
你就不能在狱中再对我发狠。

你还会发狠的，我是你的囚徒，
我和我的一切必然任你摆布。

Sonnet 134

So now I have confessed that he is thine,

And I myself am mortgaged to thy will,

Myself I'll forfeit, so that other mine,

Thou wilt restore to be my comfort still.

But thou wilt not, nor he will not be free,

For thou art covetous, and he is kind;

He learned but surety-like to write for me

Under that bond that him as fist doth bind.

The statute of thy beauty thou wilt take,

Thou usurer that put'st forth all to use,

And sue a friend came debtor for my sake,

So him I lose through my unkind abuse.

Him I have lost, thou hast both him and me;

He pays the whole, and yet I am not free.

一三四

因此，现在我既承认他属于你，
并照你的意旨把我当抵押品，
我情愿让你把我没收，好教你
释放另一个我来宽慰我的心。

但你不肯放，他又不愿被释放，
因为你贪得无厌，他心肠又软；
他作为保人签字在那证券上，
为了开脱我，反而把自己紧拴。

分毫不放过的高利贷者，你将要
行使你的美丽赐给你的特权
去控诉那为我而负债的知交；
于是我失去他，因为把他欺骗。

我把他失掉，你却占有他和我。
他还清了债，我依然不得开脱。

Sonnet 135

Whoever hath her wish, thou hast thy Will,

And Will to boot, and Will in overplus;

More than enough am I that vex thee still,

To thy sweet will making addition thus.

Wilt thou, whose will is large and spacious,

Not once vouchsafe to hide my will in thine?

Shall will in others seem right gracious,

And in my will no fair acceptance shine?

The sea, all water, yet receives rain still,

And in abundance addeth to his store;

So thou being rich in will add to thy Will

One will of mine to make thy large Will more.

Let no unkind, no fair beseechers kill;

Think all but one, and me in that one Will.

一三五

假如女人有满足，你就得如"愿"，
还有额外的心愿，多到数不清；
而多余的我总是要把你纠缠，
想在你心愿的花上添我的锦。

你的心愿汪洋无边，难道不能
容我把我的心愿在里面隐埋？
难道别人的心愿都那么可亲，
而我的心愿就不配你的青睐？

大海，满满是水，照样承受雨点，
好把它的贮藏品大量地增加；
多心愿的你，就该把我的心愿
添上，使你的心愿得到更扩大。

别让无情的"不"把求爱者窒息；
让众愿同一愿，而我就在这愿里。

Sonnet 136

If thy soul check thee that I come so near,

Swear to thy blind soul that I was thy 'Will',

And will, thy soul knows, is admitted there;

Thus far for love, my love-suit, sweet, fulfil.

'Will' will fulfil the treasure of thy love,

Ay, fill it full with wills, and my will one,

In things of great receipt with case we prove

Among a number one is reckoned none.

Then in the number let me pass untold,

Though in thy store's account I one must be;

For nothing hold me, so it please thee hold

That nothing me, a something sweet to thee.

Make but my name thy love, and love that still,

And then thou lovest me, for my name is Will.

一三六

你的灵魂若骂你我走得太近，
请对你那瞎灵魂说我是你"心愿"，
而"心愿"，她晓得，对她并非陌生；
为了爱，让我的爱如愿吧，心肝。

心愿将充塞你的爱情的宝藏，
请用心愿充满它，把我算一个，
须知道宏大的容器非常便当，
多装或少装一个算不了什么。

请容许我混在队伍中间进去，
不管怎样说我总是其中之一；
把我看作微末不足道，但必须
把这微末看作你心爱的东西。

把我名字当你的爱，始终如一，
就是爱我，因为"心愿"是我的名字。

Sonnet 137

Thou blind fool, Love, what dost thou to mine eyes,

That they behold, and see not what they see?

They know what beauty is, see where it lies,

Yet what the best is take the worst to be.

If eyes corrupt by over-partial looks

Be anchored in the bay where all men ride,

Why of eyes' falsehood hast thou forged hooks,

Whereto the judgment of my heart is tied?

Why should my heart think that a several plot

Which my heart knows the wide world's common place?

Or mine eyes seeing this, say this is not,

To put fair truth upon so foul a face?

In things right true my heart and eyes have erred,

And to this false plague are they now transferred.

一三七

又瞎又蠢的爱，你对我的眸子
干了什么，以致它们视而不见？
它们认得美，也看见美在哪里，
却居然错把那极恶当作至善。

我的眼睛若受了偏见的歪扭，
在那人人行驶的海湾里下锚，
你为何把它们的虚妄作成钩，
把我的心的判断力钩得牢牢？

难道是我的心，明知那是公地，
硬把它当作私人游乐的花园？
还是我眼睛否认明显的事实，
硬拿美丽的真蒙住丑恶的脸？

我的心和眼既迷失了真方向，
自然不得不陷入虚妄的膏肓。

Sonnet 138

When my love swears that she is made of truth,

I do believe her, though I know she lies,

That she might think me some untutored youth,

Unlearned in the world's false subtleties.

Thus vainly thinking that she thinks me young.

Although she knows my days are past the best,

Simply I credit her false-speaking tongue,

On both sides thus is simple truth suppressed.

But wherefore says she not she is unjust?

And wherefore say not I that I am old?

O! love's best habit is in seeming trust,

And age in love loves not to have years told.

Therefore I lie with her and she with me,

And in our faults by lies we flattered be.

一三八

我爱人赌咒说她浑身是忠实，
我相信她（虽然明知她在撒谎），
让她认为我是个无知的孩子，
不懂得世间种种骗人的勾当。

于是我就妄想她当我还年轻，
虽然明知我盛年已一去不复返；
她的油嘴滑舌我天真地信任：
这样，纯朴的真话双方都隐瞒。

但是为什么她不承认说假话？
为什么我又不承认我已经衰老？
爱的习惯是连信任也成欺诈，
老年谈恋爱最怕把年龄提到。

因此，我既欺骗她，她也欺骗我，
咱俩的爱情就在欺骗中作乐。

Sonnet 139

O, call not me to justify the wrong

That thy unkindness lays upon my heart;

Wound me not with thine eye but with thy tongue;

Use power with power, and slay me not by art.

Tell me thou lov'st elsewhere, but in my sight,

Dear heart, forbear to glance thine eye aside:

What need'st thou wound with cunning when thy might

Is more than my o'er-pressed defence can bide?

Let me excuse thee: ah! my love well knows

Her pretty looks have been mine enemies,

And therefore from my face she turns my foes,

That they elsewhere might dart their injuries.

Yet do not so; but since I am near slain,

Kill me outright with looks and rid my pain.

一三九

哦，别叫我原谅你的残酷不仁
对于我的心的不公正的冒犯；
请用舌头伤害我，可别用眼睛；
狠狠打击我，杀我，可别耍手段。

说你已爱上了别人；但当我面，
心肝，可别把眼睛向旁边张望。
何必要耍手段，既然你的强权
已够打垮我过分紧张的抵抗？

让我替你辩解说："我爱人明知
她那明媚的流盼是我的死仇，
才把我的敌人从我脸上转移，
让它向别处放射害人的毒镞！"

可别这样。我已经一息奄奄，
不如一下盯死我，解除了苦难。

Sonnet 140

Be wise as thou art cruel, do not press

My tongue-tied patience with too much disdain;

Lest sorrow lend me words and words express

The manner of my pity-wanting pain.

If I might teach thee wit, better it were,

Though not to love, yet, love, to tell me so;

As testy sick men, when their deaths be near,

No news but health from their physicians know;

For if I should despair, I should grow mad,

And in my madness might speak ill of thee,

Now this ill-wresting world is grown so bad,

Mad slanderers by mad ears believed be,

That I may not be so, nor thou belied,

Bear thine eyes straight, though thy proud heart go wide.

一四〇

你狠心，也该放聪明；别让侮蔑
把我不作声的忍耐逼得太甚；
免得悲哀赐我喉舌，让你领略
我的可怜的痛苦会怎样发狠。

你若学了乖，爱呵，就觉得理应
对我说你爱我，纵使你不如此；
好像暴躁的病人，当死期已近，
只愿听医生报告健康的消息。

因为我若是绝望，我就会发疯，
疯狂中难保不把你胡乱咒骂。
这乖张世界是那么不成体统，
疯狂的耳总爱听疯子的坏话。

要我不发疯，而你不遭受诽谤，
你得把眼睛正视，尽管心放荡。

Sonnet 141

In faith, I do not love thee with mine eyes,

For they in thee a thousand errors note;

But 'tis my heart that loves what they despise,

Who, in despite of view, is pleased to dote.

Nor are mine cars with thy tongue's tune delighted;

Nor tender feeling, to base touches prone.

Nor taste nor smell desire to be invited

To any sensual feast with thee alone.

But my five wits nor my five senses can

Dissuade one foolish heart from serving thee,

Who leaves unswayed the likeness of a man,

Thy proud heart's slave and vassal wretch to be.

Only my plague thus far I count my gain,

That she that makes me sin, awards me pain.

一四一

说实话，我的眼睛并不喜欢你，
它们发现你身上百孔和千疮；
但眼睛瞧不起的，心儿却着迷，
它一味溺爱，不管眼睛怎样想。

我耳朵也不觉得你嗓音好听，
就是我那容易受刺激的触觉，
或味觉，或嗅觉，都不见得高兴
参加你身上任何官能的盛酌。

可是无论我五种机智或五官
都不能劝阻痴心去把你侍奉，
我昂藏的丈夫仪表它再不管，
只甘愿做你傲慢的心的仆从。

不过我的灾难也非全无好处：
她引诱我犯罪，也教会我受苦。

Sonnet 142

Love is my sin and thy dear virtue hate,

Hate of my sin, grounded on sinful loving,

O, but with mine, compare thou thine own state,

And thou shalt find it merits not reproving;

Or, if it do, not from those lips of thine,

That have profaned their scarlet ornaments

And sealed false bonds of love as oft as mine,

Robbed others' beds' revenues of their rents.

Be it lawful I love thee, as thou lov'st those

Whom thine eyes woo as mine importune thee,

Root pity in thy heart that when it grows

Thy pity may deserve to pitied be.

If thou dost seek to have what thou dost hide,

By self-example mayst thou be denied.

一四二

我的罪咎是爱，你的美德是憎，
你憎我的罪，为了我多咎的爱。
哦，你只要比一比你我的实情，
就会发觉责备我多么不应该。

就算应该，也不能出自你嘴唇，
因为它们亵渎过自己的口红，
劫夺过别人床笫应得的租金，
和我一样屡次偷订爱的假盟。

我爱你，你爱他们，都一样正当，
尽管你追求他们而我讨你厌。
让哀怜的种子在你心里暗长，
终有天你的哀怜也得人哀怜。

假如你只知追求，自己却吝啬，
你自己的榜样就会招来拒绝。

Sonnet 143

Lo! as a careful huswife runs to catch

One of her feathered creatures broke away,

Sets down her babe and makes all swift dispatch

In pursuit of the thing she would have stay,

Whilst her neglected child holds her in chase,

Cries to catch her whose busy care is bent

To follow that which flies before her face,

Not prizing her poor infant's discontent;

So run'st thou after that which flies from thee,

Whilst I thy babe chase thee afar behind;

But if thou catch thy hope, turn back to me,

And play the mother's part, kiss me, be kind.

So will I pray that thou mayst have thy Will,

If thou turn back, and my loud crying still.

一四三

看呀，像一个小心翼翼的主妇
跑着去追撵一只逃走的母鸡，
把孩子扔下，拼命快跑，要抓住
那个她急着要得回来的东西；

被扔下的孩子紧跟在她后头，
哭哭啼啼要赶上她，而她只管
望前一直追撵，一步也不停留，
不顾她那可怜的小孩的不满。

同样，你追那个逃避你的家伙，
而我（你的孩子）却在后头追你；
你若赶上了希望，请回头照顾我，
尽妈妈的本分，轻轻吻我，很和气。

只要你回头来抚慰我的悲啼，
我就会祷告神让你从心所欲。

Sonnet 144

Two loves I have of comfort and despair,
Which like two spirits do suggest me still,
The better angel is a man right fair,
The worser spirit a woman coloured ill.

To win me soon to hell, my female evil
Tempteth my better angel from my side,
And would corrupt my saint to be a devil,
Wooing his purity with her foul pride.

And whether that my angel be turned fiend,
Suspect I may, yet not directly tell;
But being both from me, both to each friend,
I guess one angel in another's hell.

Yet this shall I never know, but live in doubt,
Till my bad angel fire my good one out.

一四四

两个爱人像精灵般把我诱惑，
一个叫安慰，另外一个叫绝望。
善的天使是个男子，丰姿绰约；
恶的幽灵是个女人，其貌不扬。

为了促使我早进地狱，那女鬼
引诱我的善精灵硬把我抛开，
还要把他迷惑，使沦落为妖魅，
用肮脏的骄傲追求纯洁的爱。

我的天使是否已变成了恶魔，
我无法一下子确定，只能猜疑；
但两个都把我扔下，互相结合，
一个想必进了另一个的地狱。

可是这一点我永远无法猜透，
除非是恶的天使把善的撵走。

Sonnet 145

Those lips that Love's own hand did make,

Breathed forth the sound that said 'I hate'

To me that languished for her sake;

But when she saw my woeful state,

Straight in her heart did mercy come,

Chiding that tongue that ever sweet

Was used in giving gentle doom,

And taught it thus anew to greet:

'I hate' she altered with an end,

That followed it as gentle day

Doth follow night, who like a fiend

From heaven to hell is flown away;

'I hate', from hate away she threw,

And saved my life saying 'not you'.

一四五

爱神亲手捏就的嘴唇
对着为她而憔悴的我，
吐出了这声音说，"我恨"。
但是她一看见我难过，

心里就马上大发慈悲，
责备那一向都是用来
宣布甜蜜的判词的嘴，
教它要把口气改过来。

"我恨"，她又把尾巴补缀，
那简直像明朗的白天
赶走了魔鬼似的黑夜，
把它从天堂甩进阴间。

她把"我恨"的恨字摒弃，
救了我的命说，"不是你"。

Sonnet 146

Poor soul, the centre of my sinful earth,

Thrall to these rebel powers that thee array;

Why dost thou pine within and suffer dearth,

Painting thy outward walls so costly gay?

Why so large cost, having so short a lease,

Dost thou upon thy fading mansion spend?

Shall worms, inheritors of this excess,

Eat up thy charge? is this thy body's end?

Then soul, live thou upon thy servant's loss,

And let that pine to aggravate thy store;

Buy terms divine in selling hours of dross;

Within be fed, without be rich no more:

So shall thou feed on Death, that feeds on men,

And Death once dead, there's no more dying then.

一四六

可怜的灵魂，万恶身躯的中心，
被围攻你的叛逆势力所俘掳，
为何在暗中憔悴，忍受着饥馑，
却把外壁妆得那么堂皇丽都？

赁期那么短，这倾颓中的大厦
难道还值得你这样铺张浪费？
是否要让蛆虫来继承这奢华，
把它吃光？这可是肉体的依皈？

所以，灵魂，请拿你仆人来度日，
让他消瘦，以便充实你的贮藏，
拿无用时间来兑换永欠租期，
让内心得滋养，别管外表堂皇。

这样，你将吃掉那吃人的死神，
而死神一死，世上就永无死人。

Sonnet 147

My love is as a fever, longing still

For that which longer nurseth the disease,

Feeding on that which doth preserve the ill,

The uncertain sickly appetite to please.

My reason, the physician to my love,

Angry that his prescriptions are not kept,

Hath left me, and I desperate now approve

Desire is death, which physic did except.

Past cure I am, now reason is past care,

And frantic-mad with evermore unrest;

My thoughts and my discourse as mad men's are,

At random from the truth vainly expressed;

For I have sworn thee fair and thought thee bright,

Who art as black as hell, as dark as night.

一四七

我的爱是一种热病，它老切盼
那能够使它长期保养的单方，
服食一种能维持病状的药散，
使多变的病态食欲长久盛旺。

理性（那医治我的爱情的医生）
生气我不遵守他给我的嘱咐，
把我扔下，使我绝望，因为不信
医药的欲望，我知道，是条死路。

我再无生望，既然丧失了理智，
整天都惶惑不安、烦躁、疯狂；
无论思想或谈话，全像个疯子，
脱离了真实，无目的，杂乱无章。

因为我曾赌咒说你美，说你璀璨，
你却是地狱一般黑，夜一般暗。

Sonnet 148

O me, what eyes hath Love put in my head,

Which have no correspondence with true sight!

Or, if they have, where is my judgment fled,

That censures falsely what they see aright?

If that be fair whereon my false eyes dote,

What means the world to say it is not so?

If it be not, then love doth well denote

Love's eye is not so true as all men's. No,

How can it? O, how can Love's eye be true,

That is so vexed with watching and with tears?

No marvel then, though I mistake my view;

The sun itself sees not, till heaven clears.

O cunning Love! with tears thou keep'st me blind,

Lest eyes well-seeing thy foul faults should find.

一四八

唉，爱把什么眼睛装在我脑里，
使我完全认不清真正的景象？
说认得清吧，理智又去了哪里，[①]
　竟错判了眼睛所见到的真相？

如果我眼睛所迷恋的真是美，
为何大家都异口同声不承认？
若真不美呢，那就绝对无可讳，
　爱情的眼睛不如一般人看得真。

当然喽，它怎能够，爱眼怎能够
看得真呢，它日夜都泪水汪汪？
那么，我看不准又怎算得稀有？
太阳也要等天晴才照得明亮。

狡猾的爱神！你用泪把我弄瞎，
只因怕明眼把你的丑恶揭发。

---

① 此处文字原稿缺失（第三行），由编者据其他译本补充。

Sonnet 149

Canst thou, O cruel! say I love thee not,

When I against myself with thee partake?

Do I not think on thee, when I forgot

Am of myself, all tyrant, for thy sake?

Who hateth thee that I do call my friend?

On whom frown'st thou that I do fawn upon?

Nay,[①] if thou lour'st on me, do I not spend

Revenge upon myself with present moan?

What merit do I in myself respect,

That is so proud thy service to despise,

When all my best doth worship thy defect,

Commanded by the motion of thine eyes?

But, love, hate on, for now I know thy mind;

Those that can see thou lov'st, and I am blind.

---

① 〈古〉副词：不，否（=no）。

一四九

你怎能，哦，狠心的，否认我爱你，
当我和你协力把我自己厌恶？
我不是在想念你，当我为了你
完全忘掉我自己，哦，我的暴主？

我可曾把那恨你的人当朋友？
我可曾对你厌恶的人献殷勤？
不仅这样，你对我一皱起眉头，
我不是马上叹气，把自己痛恨？

我还有什么可以自豪的优点，
傲慢到不屑于为你服役奔命，
既然我的美都崇拜你的缺陷，
唯你的眼波的流徙转移是听？

但，爱呵，尽管憎吧，我已猜透你：
你爱那些明眼的，而我是瞎子。

Sonnet 150

O, from what power hast thou this powerful might

With insufficiency my heart to sway?

To make me give the lie to my true sight,

And swear that brightness doth not grace the day?

Whence hast thou this becoming of things ill,

That in the very refuse of thy deeds,

There is such strength and warrantise of skill

That, in my mind, thy worst all best exceeds?

Who taught thee how to make me love thee more

The more I hear and see just cause of hate?

O, though I love what others do abhor,

With others thou shouldst not abhor my state:

If thy unworthiness raised love in me,

More worthy I to be beloved of thee.

一五〇

哦，从什么威力你取得这力量，
连缺陷也能把我的心灵支配？
教我诬蔑我可靠的目光撒谎，
并矢口否认太阳使白天明媚？

何来这化臭腐为神奇的本领，
使你的种种丑恶不堪的表现
都具有一种灵活强劲的保证，
使它们，对于我，超越一切至善？

谁教你有办法使我更加爱你，
当我听到和见到你种种可憎？
哦，尽管我钟爱着人家所嫌弃，
你总不该嫌弃我，同人家一条心。

既然你越不可爱，越使得我爱，
你就该觉得我更值得你喜爱。

Sonnet 151

Love is too young to know what conscience is;

Yet who knows not conscience is born of love?

Then, gentle cheater, urge not my amiss,

Lest guilty of my faults thy sweet self prove.

For, thou betraying me, I do betray

My nobler part to my gross body's treason;

My soul doth tell my body that he may

Triumph in love; flesh stays no farther reason;

But, rising at thy name, doth point out thee

As his triumphant prize. Proud of this pride,

He is contented thy poor drudge to be,

To stand in thy affairs, fall by thy side.

No want of conscience hold it that I call

Her 'love', for whose dear love I rise and fall.

一五一

爱神太年轻，不懂得良心是什么；
但谁不晓得良心是爱情所产？
那么，好骗子，就别专找我的错，
免得我的罪把温婉的你也牵连。

因为，你出卖了我，我的笨肉体
又哄我出卖我更高贵的部分；
我灵魂叮嘱我肉体，说它可以
在爱情上胜利。肉体再不作声，

一听见你的名字就马上指出
你是它的胜利品；它趾高气扬，
死心踏地做你最鄙贱的家奴，
任你颐指气使，或倒在你身旁。

所以我可问心无愧地称呼她
做"爱"，我为她的爱起来又倒下。

Sonnet 152

In loving thee thou know'st I am forsworn,

But thou art twice forsworn, to me love swearing,

In act thy bed-vow broke and new faith torn,

In vowing new hate after new love bearing.

But why of two oaths' breach do I accuse thee,

When I break twenty? I am perjured most;

For all my vows are oaths but to misuse thee

And all my honest faith in thee is lost.

For I have sworn deep oaths of thy deep kindness,

Oaths of thy love, thy truth, thy constancy,

And, to enlighten thee, gave eyes to blindness,

Or made them swear against the thing they see;

For I have sworn thee fair: more perjured I,

To swear against the truth so foul a lie!

一五二

你知道我对你的爱并不可靠，
但你赌咒爱我，这话更靠不住；
你撕掉床头盟，又把新约毁掉，
既结了新欢，又种下新的憎恶。

但我为什么责备你两番背盟，
自己却背了二十次！最反复是我。
我对你一切盟誓都只是滥用，
因而对于你已经失尽了信约。

我曾矢口作证你对我的深爱，
说你多热烈、多忠诚、永不变卦，
我使眼睛失明，好让你显光彩，
教眼睛发誓，把眼前景说成虚假——

我发誓说你美！还有比这荒唐：
抹煞真理去坚持那么黑的谎！

Sonnet 153

Cupid laid by his brand, and fell asleep:
A maid of Dian's this advantage found,
And his love-kindling fire did quickly steep
In a cold valley-fountain of that ground;

Which borrowed from this holy fire of Love
A dateless lively heat, still to endure,
And grew a seeting bath, which yet men prove
Against strange maladies a sovereign cure.

But at my mistress' eye Love's brand new-fired,
The boy for trial needs would touch my breast;
I, sick withal, the help of bath desired,
And thither hied, a sad distempered guest,

But found no cure: the bath for my help lies
Where Cupid got new fire—my mistress' eyes.

一五三

爱神放下他的火炬，沉沉睡去：
月神的一个仙女乘了这机会
赶快把那枝煽动爱火的火炬
浸入山间一道冷冰冰的泉水。

泉水，既从这神圣的火炬得来
一股不灭的热，就永远在燃烧，
变成了沸腾的泉，一直到现在
还证实具有起死回生的功效。

但这火炬又在我情妇眼里点火，
为了试验，爱神碰一下我胸口，
我马上不舒服，又急躁又难过，
一刻不停地跑向温泉去求救。

但全不见效：能治好我的温泉
只有新燃起爱火的、我情人的眼。

Sonnet 154

The little Love-god lying once asleep

Laid by his side his heart-inflaming brand,

Whilst many nymphs that vowed chaste life to keep

Came tripping by; but in her maiden hand

The fairest votary took up that fire

Which many legions of true hearts had warmed;

And so the general of hot desire

Was sleeping by a virgin hand disarmed.

This brand she quenched in a cool well by,

Which from Love's fire took heat perpetual,

Growing a bath and healthful remedy

For men discased; but I, my mistress' thrall,

Came there for cure, and this by that I prove,

Love's fire heats water, water cools not love.

Ingres Del.
à Madame
Marcotte

一五四

小小爱神有一次呼呼地睡着，
把点燃心焰的火炬放在一边，
一群蹁跹的贞洁的仙女恰巧
走过；其中最美的一个天仙

用她处女的手把那曾经烧红
万千颗赤心的火炬偷偷拿走，
于是这玩火小法师在酣睡中
便缴械给那贞女的纤纤素手。

她把火炬往附近冷泉里一浸，
泉水被爱神的烈火烧得沸腾，
变成了温泉，能消除人间百病；
但我呵，被我情妇播弄得头疼，

跑去温泉就医，才把这点弄清：
爱烧热泉水，泉水冷不了爱情。

《爱的教育》
湖南文艺出版社
ISBN：9787540446840
开本：32开/定价：25.00元
意大利政府官方授权名家
权威版本 意大利原版完整
插图
荣获意大利驻华使馆颁发
的"意大利政府文化奖"

《飞鸟集·新月集》
湖南文艺出版社
ISBN：9787540447243
开本：32开/定价：22.00元
每天读一句泰戈尔，忘却
世上一切苦痛
首位荣获诺贝尔文学奖的
东方诗哲、"亚洲第一诗
人"泰戈尔传世佳作

《假如给我三天光明》
湖南文艺出版社
ISBN：9787540447984
开本：32开/定价：22.00元
人类意志力最伟大的典范
作品
一本向光明、智慧、希
望、仁爱引航的人生手册
世界文学史上无与伦比的
杰作

《再别康桥·人间四月天》
湖南文艺出版社
ISBN：9787540447922
开本：32开/定价：25.00元
新月派代表诗人&民国第
一才女 诗歌精选 首度合
集出版
穿越半个多世纪的心灵交
会，值得一生珍藏的绝美
诗篇

《朝花夕拾》
湖南文艺出版社
ISBN：9787540448103
开本：32开/定价：20.00元
一位文化巨人的回忆记事
一幅清末民初的生活画卷
描绘鲁迅先生世界的唯一
作品

《落花生》
湖南文艺出版社
ISBN：9787540448097
开本：32开/定价：22.00元
被忽视的文学大师许地山
的传世散文名作
全新彩绘插图，让蒙尘的
珍珠重现光华

《背影》
湖南文艺出版社
ISBN：9787540448080
开本：32开/定价：25.00元
白话美文典范，"天地间
第一等至情文学"
散文杰作&诗歌名篇 收藏
一个最完整的朱自清

《伊索寓言》
湖南文艺出版社
ISBN：9787540448561
开本：32开/定价：25.00元
影响人类文化的100本书之一
世界上拥有最多读者的寓
言始祖
特别奉送19世纪大师杜雷
百幅原版精美插图

《呼兰河传》
湖南文艺出版社
ISBN：9787540448448
开本：32开/定价：22.00元
一个天才作家奉献给人间
的礼物
穿越时光的艺术珍品
一代才女萧红代表作

《雾都孤儿》
湖南文艺出版社
ISBN：9787540448493
开本：32开/定价：26.00元
英国现实主义文学的杰出
代表作
中国译协"资深翻译家"
权威全译
原版经典插图，拂去岁月
尘埃，让爱与希望历久弥新

《春风沉醉的晚上》
湖南文艺出版社
ISBN: 9787540448509
开本: 32开/定价: 25.00元
郁达夫中短篇小说精选集
感伤的浪漫, 率真的反叛
成就现代文坛永不沉沦的
经典之作

《春醪集》
湖南文艺出版社
ISBN: 9787540448554
开本: 32开/定价: 23.00元
偷饮香美春醪的年轻人,
醉中做出的几许好梦
现代中国散文的奇异之作,
"中国的兰姆"昙花般的
青春絮语

《城南旧事》
中国画报出版社
ISBN: 9787802208056
开本: 32开/定价: 24.80元
名家林海音独步文坛三十
多年的经典作品
入选二十世纪中文小说
一百强
上海是张爱玲的, 北京是
林海音的。

《美国悲剧》（上、下册）
湖南文艺出版社
开本: 32开/定价: 58.00元
美国小说黄金时代的经典
力作
美国现代文学三巨头之一
代表作
"美国发财梦牺牲者"的
一代悲剧

《珍妮姑娘》
湖南文艺出版社
ISBN: 9787540448820
开本: 32开/定价: 28.00元
一曲悲天悯人的恸歌
美国小说黄金时代的经典
力作
美国现代文学三巨头之一
成名作

《嘉莉妹妹》
湖南文艺出版社
ISBN: 9787540448813
开本: 32开/定价: 32.00元
掀开美国小说黄金时代序
幕的经典力作
美国现代文学三巨头之一
成名作
美国小说中一座具有历史
意义的里程碑

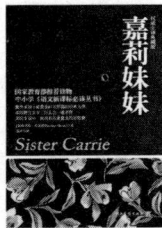

《猎人笔记》
湖南文艺出版社
ISBN: 9787540448912
开本: 32开/定价: 28.00元
俄国现实主义艺术大师的
成名之作
俄国文学史上"一部点燃
火种的书"

《格列佛游记》
湖南文艺出版社
ISBN: 9787540448530
开本: 32开/定价: 23.00元
世界文学史上极具童话色彩
的讽刺小说
离奇荒诞的航海游记, 犀利
幽默的政治寓言

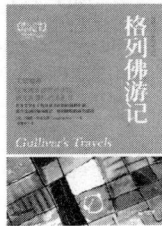

《鲁滨孙漂流记》
湖南文艺出版社
ISBN: 9787540448752
开本: 32开/定价: 25.00元
倾注勇气的冒险之旅, 锐
意进取的孤岛求生记
震撼欧洲文学史的惊世作品

《哈姆雷特》
湖南文艺出版社
ISBN: 9787540448578
开本: 32开/定价: 20.00元
在他身上, 我们看到作为一
个人的全部复杂
莎翁经典名作, 世界戏剧史
上的钻石篇章

《十四行诗》
湖南文艺出版社
开本：32开/定价：25.00元
你从未见过的"甜蜜的莎士比亚"
时光流转中爱的不朽箴言
莎翁在世时唯一诗集
"中国拜伦"梁宗岱经典译本

《最后一课》
湖南文艺出版社
ISBN：9787540449209
开本：32开/定价：22.00元
感受都德带给你心灵的震撼和美轮美奂的诗意
脍炙人口的名篇
入选多国中小学语文教材

《缀网劳蛛:许地山小说菁华集》
湖南文艺出版社
开本：32开/定价：23.00元
被忽视的文学大师许地山的传世小说名作
抒写人性之美的一枝奇葩

《子夜》
湖南文艺出版社
ISBN：9787540449285
开本：32开/定价：28.00元
"中国第一部写实主义的成功的长篇小说"
被评为"可以与《追忆似水年华》《百年孤独》媲美的杰作"

《汤姆·索亚历险记》
湖南文艺出版社
ISBN：9787540449117
开本：32开/定价：22.00元
"美国文学史上的林肯"
献给所有孩子和大人的礼物
一段五彩斑斓的少年成长史
一部险象环生的冒险传奇

《格兰特船长的儿女》
湖南文艺出版社
ISBN：9787540449230
开本：32开/定价：28.00元
"现代科学幻想小说之父"令人惊异的科学预言
"海洋三部曲"首作
百科全书式对大自然的奇思妙想

《海底两万里》
湖南文艺出版社
开本：32开/定价：28.00元
最具魔力的科幻小说经典
充满自由与孤独的深海之旅

《神秘岛》
湖南文艺出版社
ISBN：9787540449223
开本：32开/定价：28.00元
"现代科学幻想小说之父"令人惊异的科学预言
"海洋三部曲"第三部
多姿多彩想象力的伟大尝试

《羊脂球》
湖南文艺出版社
ISBN：9787540449292
开本：32开/定价：25.00元
在他笔下，世人可叹可笑，寒冷入木三分
爱情至死不渝，欲望活色生香
法国"短篇小说之王"莫泊桑代表作全记录